AF697455

THE POLITICS OF MEDICARE
WHO GETS WHAT, WHEN AND HOW

Gwendolyn Gray is a senior lecturer in political science at the Australian National University. She specialises in Australian politics and public policy in comparative perspective. A nurse in her first career, she has studied and written on the Australian and overseas health systems for over twenty years.

BRIEFINGS

A series of topical books exploring social, political and cultural issues in contemporary Australia

Series editors: Peter Browne and Julian Thomas, Institute for Social Research, Swinburne University of Technology

Also in this series

America's Pie: Trade and Culture Since 9/11
by Jock Given

Slapping on the Writs:
Defamation, Developers and Community Activism
by Brian Walters

Sexing it Up: Iraq, Intelligence and Australia
by Geoffrey Barker

Refuge Australia: Australia's Humanitarian Record
by Klaus Neumann

Rebels with a Cause: Independents in Australian Politics
by Brian Costar & Jennifer Curtin

The Case for an Australian Bill of Rights: Freedom in the War on Terror
by George Williams

The Politics of Medicare

WHO GETS WHAT, WHEN AND HOW

GWENDOLYN GRAY

RA
412
.5
A8
G73
2004

WITHDRAWN

UNSW
PRESS

b# 230952

A UNSW Press book

Published by
University of New South Wales Press Ltd
University of New South Wales
Sydney NSW 2052
AUSTRALIA
www.unswpress.com.au

© Gwendolyn Gray 2004
First published 2004

This book is copyright. Apart from any fair dealing for the purpose of private study, research, criticism or review, as permitted under the Copyright Act, no part may be reproduced by any process without written permission. Enquiries should be addressed to the publisher.

National Library of Australia
Cataloguing-in-Publication entry

Gray, Gwendolyn.

The politics of Medicare: who gets what, when and how.

ISBN 0 86840 703 8.

1. Medicare (Australia). 2. Insurance, Health – Australia. 3. Medical care – Australia. I. Title. (Series: Briefings series).

368.4200994

Cover photograph: Darren England/Newspix

Printed by BPA Digital

Contents

In memory of my father,
Albert Edward Jamieson,
and for Emmy and Maddy

Preface

This book identifies the fundamental forces driving Australian health politics. It explores the way these forces have operated in recent conflicts and assesses the implications of present policy directions. My aim is to provide readers with information with which to evaluate health debates, including those that were high on the political agenda in 2003 and continue to capture headlines in 2004 and beyond. My main argument is that the health system, as reshaped by the Howard government, cannot work. The combination of Medicare and a large private sector is a highly unstable arrangement which cannot survive. Eventually, the Commonwealth will be forced either to spend even more tax money to subsidise private insurance or to abolish Medicare altogether.

The politics of Australian health policy can be viewed as an enduring struggle between diametrically opposed interests – a struggle over who is to get what, when and how. Powerful provider interests, hostile to public control, occupy one side of the arena. On the other side are consumers, most of whom benefit from public involvement in the health industry and from publicly provided services which, as individuals, they cannot provide for themselves. In most countries, political parties have taken a bipartisan approach and governments have placed themselves somewhere between these two sets of interests, negotiating an accommodation. Not so in Australia, where the two major political parties are on opposite sides of the struggle and major change has become a motif of the system.

For over 50 years, Australian health policy has oscillated backwards and forwards between systems of private and public health insurance.

Each time a Labor government has introduced a public scheme, an incoming Coalition government has dismantled it. Radical change of this magnitude is unique: nowhere in the OECD have major programs been introduced and terminated with every change of national government. And in no other country have governments used taxpayer funds to directly subsidise private health insurance costs, predominantly for the benefit of wealthier members of the community. The Howard government has followed in the footsteps of its predecessors. Like the Fraser government before it, it was elected on a promise to maintain Medicare but it has steadily privatised the system, with serious implications for access, equity and cost control.

As the next federal election approaches, obfuscation surrounds the position of both major parties. The Howard government claims to be strengthening Medicare but clearly remains committed to a predominantly private system. The Labor Party voices support for universality but, in 1998, participated in the introduction of a taxpayer-funded private insurance rebate, firmly entrenching a two-tiered system. Nor has Labor yet committed itself to redirect the rebate money to Medicare, despite calls from consumer and welfare groups to do so. Thus, we may be witnessing the end of a very long struggle to gain universal access to hospital and medical services. When Labor next returns to office, it may not reinstate Medicare.

In two-tiered systems with multiple payment agencies, health financing arrangements are complex. And in Australia, they are becoming more complex every day, as the government tries to patch up its shaky system with special arrangements, such as safety net schemes. One of the reasons political parties and interest groups are able to obfuscate is that a considerable investment of time is needed to understand how the system works. I have written this book in the hope that it will go some small way towards shedding light on the jostling for position that has characterised Australian health policy for more than a century.

The work of a number of health policy analysts in Canada, the United States, Britain and Australia has influenced my thinking. Reference to this work, without which I could not have written this book, is found in the chapter notes at the end of this book. Especially, I thank Canadian policymakers, academics and health professionals for the time they have so generously made available for discussions over the past twenty years. I wish to thank Jill Stenhouse, Pam Molloy and Roy Harvey for reading and commenting on parts of the manuscript and Peter Howe for providing me with emergency research assistance and an excellent clippings service.

Introduction

Health service planning... has been described as "planning by decibels" because powerful vested interests dominate the policy-making process.

– SIDNEY SAX, 1984

Health policy conflicts are so intractable, it has been said, that political rivals can be vanquished simply by giving them responsibility for the portfolio. Since the emergence of modern medicine towards the end of the nineteenth century, health ministers in Australia, as in most industrialised countries, have been regularly embroiled in do-or-die struggles between unyielding interests. Health has been a major issue at almost every federal election since the 1940s and disputes have raged between elections. Nowhere is Harold Lasswell's view of politics as a struggle over who gets what, when and how more clearly exemplified than in the politics of health policy.[1]

Huge benefits flow from the production of health services, and the shape of a nation's health system largely determines who gains and who loses. Health is big business. Average spending in OECD countries was 8.4 per cent of gross domestic product in 2001. Australia's spending in the same year was 9.2 per cent of GDP; in the country with the highest costs, the United States, expenditure was 13.9 per cent of GDP.[2] The enormous size of health as an industry can be illustrated by a comparison with defence: in 2001, Australia spent well over five times as much on health as on defence; in the United States health spending was four-and-a-half times higher than defence spending.[3] For providers, high profits and high incomes are at stake. For citizens, the central question is whether access to high-quality and appropriate services is affordable. And governments have their own set of concerns: ideology, electoral advantage and issues of principle are important but, throughout the OECD, the overriding government objective of the past two decades has been to restrain escalating health care costs. These three sets of objectives – high profits and incomes, affordable access to quality services and control of total health care expenditures – cannot all be achieved at the same time. The stakes, therefore, are high. Nowhere, with perhaps the exception of the United States, have health financing policies been more vehemently contested than in Australia.

In keeping with the tradition of perpetual struggle, 2003 was a troubled year in Australian health policy. Continuing anxiety about declining levels of general practitioner bulk billing manifested itself in lively political activity from the beginning. As the primary instrument for removing the financial barriers that prevent people from using medical services, bulk billing is a fundamental building block of Medicare. By the end of the year, little had been achieved: the government's efforts to defuse health policy as a political issue had failed. And the passage of the revamped Medicare Plus in March 2004 has done nothing to resolve the main problems of the system.

Public disquiet intensified when, in February 2003, an ACNielsen poll found that bulk billing had declined sharply and predicted that, within six months, only 22 per cent of general practitioners would offer this payment method for all services.[4] When the prime minister claimed in March that bulk billing was never meant to be universal he set off another round of argument; "leaks" about proposed reforms served only to magnify the controversy. The announcement of the Fairer Medicare reform package at the end of April 2003 pleased no one. It was condemned by all major stakeholders, provider and consumer groups alike, and all the other political parties. The Labor opposition pledged a double injection of funding to "revive" Medicare.

In the meantime, "defend Medicare" groups formed around the country and existing groups stepped up their activities. Official statistics showed that general practitioner bulk billing had fallen to its lowest level in thirteen years and headlines like "Economic rationalists move in on Medicare" appeared. Leading journalists were generally critical, and some, like Alan Ramsey, claimed that the prime minister had always intended to dismantle Medicare, despite his promise in 1996 that the scheme would be retained "in its entirety."[5] Opinion polls showed that only 10 per cent of people thought they would be better off under the Fairer Medicare plan and 77 per cent of people thought that the tax cuts of the May budget should have been spent on health and education.[6] Enabling legislation failed to pass the Senate, where the Democrats moved to establish a select committee to examine Medicare issues, including the likely impact of the proposed package on access, affordability and service quality. In June, the government indicated that it was willing to negotiate with the Democrats and independents in the Senate but it was unable to secure the passage of its legislation.

Debate continued throughout the winter, fuelled by evidence from multiple perspectives presented to the Senate committee and by a report, commissioned by the Royal Australasian College of Surgeons, which found that elective surgery was increasingly being moved to private hospitals and that citizens without private insurance were being denied access to a range of surgical procedures.[7] In August, research from the Australian Institute of Health and Welfare showed that health costs had increased more than twice as fast as other prices in the previous year, reaching an all-time high of 9.3 per cent of GDP. More damaging for the government was the finding that direct charges to patients had increased even faster, by 7.7 per cent each year in real terms between 1997 and 2002, the period covering most of the government's term of office.[8] At the end of September, the prime minister announced that Tony Abbott would replace Kay Patterson as health minister.

The Senate committee, whose government members were in a minority, reported in October 2003. It concluded that the Fairer Medicare package would lead to a further decline in bulk billing for non–concession cardholders and that working families and those with chronic illnesses would be most severely affected. It recommended that the main planks of the package be rejected and that policies be developed which would be oriented "towards the role of Medicare as a universal insurer, with equal benefits for everyone."[9]

Amid the release of statistics showing a further decline in bulk billing and reports that voters rated health a priority issue, the new minister announced that he was looking at proposals to amend the package. The prime minister announced "Medicare Plus" in November. The central feature was a commitment to spend an additional $1.5 billion, to be used mainly for additional payments to doctors who continued to bulk bill concession cardholders, for more comprehensive safety nets and for additional training places for doctors and nurses. Minister Abbott announced that he was "reasonably optimistic" that the necessary legislation would be passed in the Senate within a fortnight.

He was to be disappointed. The fate of Medicare Plus, quickly tagged "Medicare Minus," by Labor leader, Simon Crean, was similar to that of the previous package. With one exception, the same array of groups condemned the new proposals because, as in the Fairer Medicare package, the assumption remained that user charges would be a permanent and major financing mechanism. The Australian Medical Association (AMA) cautiously welcomed the scheme as a "second best" option. It suggested that the money could have been better spent on an across-the-board increase in the general Medicare rebate to doctors. Minister Abbott's attempts to negotiate with the Democrats and independents in the Senate, like the efforts of his predecessor, Senator Patterson, were unsuccessful. During discussions, broader issues, such as the low bulk-billing rates among specialists, were raised, compounding problems. On 25 November, the Select Committee on Medicare was reconstituted to conduct an inquiry into key elements of Medicare Plus. The government's efforts to resolve health policy problems before 2004, an election year, had come to nothing. After intense negotiations and significant government concessions, Medicare Plus finally passed the Senate in March 2004. Because the legislation does not address the fundamental structural flaws of the two-tiered arrangements, health will continue to be a high-profile political issue.

Despite the arguments and counter-arguments, the moves and countermoves, 2003 was not an unusually contentious year in Australian health politics. Since the McGowan government tried to reform the NSW hospital system in the first years of the twentieth century, every attempt to introduce major change has been engulfed in intense controversy. Other notable periods of disputation, at times bordering on hysteria, include the proposal to introduce national health and pensions insurance in the late 1930s, Labor's attempt to introduce a national health service in the 1940s and the introduction of Medibank, Medicare's prototype, in the 1970s. In the case of Medibank, the claims that participants made and the lengths to which they were prepared to take their political activities seem extraordinary in 2004, given that national health insurance has operated for twenty years. The AMA launched a political campaign of enormous proportions. It engaged a public relations firm, placed advertisements in all sections of the media (including 250 television commercials a week) and distributed 16,000 publicity kits in 1973 alone. Doctors went on speaking tours across country and engaged the public relations services of a former Miss Australia, Sue Gallie. At the same time, every effort was made to influence members of federal parliament. The opposition spokesperson for social security, Senator Don Chipp, argued in the national legislature that the introduction of Medibank would create anarchy. "Anarchy," he said, "is a situation not unknown to socialists. It is part of their bread-and-butter."[10] The manager of the Medical Benefits Fund of Australia, a large voluntary insurance organisation, claimed that the new scheme was based on Karl Marx's theories and that health care would henceforth be bought at the "government shop."[11]

The dynamics underpinning health policy struggles are not well understood. Opinion polls, for decades, have reported that large numbers of citizens, sometimes up to 45 per cent, cannot answer straightforward questions about proposed policies, even when the issues in question are high on the political agenda. Leading journalists, too, frequently seem unclear about the details and cogency of arguments. One of the main reasons for confusion is the complexity of financing and benefit arrangements in a two-tiered system, which is being made more complicated by the day. Another reason is that contending interests push their own perspectives (often disguising them as the interests of others), making it difficult to assess their validity. As in other countries, the views of well-resourced, institutionalised provider groups tend to dominate public discussions; the voice of the community, where groups have relatively few resources, is weak. The information problem was articulated by the ABC radio presenter (and lawyer), James O'Loghlin, at the end of 2003:

> I'm still wading my way through the whole Medicare thing... It's quite embarrassing, because it's one of the big issues of the year, but I still have to go back and think, "Okay, what's the gap again, and how does that work, and how does the rebate work, and why is it if I don't have private health insurance I'm somehow worse off financially because of the rebate thing?"[12]

The main aim of the pages that follow is to fill some of this information gap. In chapter one, discussion focuses on the contending interests that populate the health policy arena. Chapter two examines an additional, and confounding, dynamic in Australian health policy: political party competition. The privatisation measures, introduced in the first two terms of the Howard government, are examined in chapter three, and the government's attempts to respond to the concerns raised by declining levels of bulk billing are discussed in chapter four. The implications, particularly for cost control, access and equity issues, of the present partially privatised Medicare system are discussed in chapters five and six. Chapter seven is a discussion of key health issues that are crowded out of Australian debates by regular and repeated wrangles over the way hospital and medical services are financed.

The conclusion, as chapter eight shows, is that the present system is inherently – and fatally – unstable. Moreover, it creates serious problems for access and equity: as doctors raise their fees and abandon bulk billing, the user charges that people pay will become both higher and more widespread, deterring people from seeking the care they need. Medicare cannot co-exist with a large private hospital insurance sector and a system in which doctors are free to choose their own fees, except at the cost of huge taxpayer subsidies to private insurance or the virtual destruction of Medicare.

Because the health debate focuses on hospital and medical services, it concentrates attention – and resources – on services for the sick. These are crucially important but they are not the only services that we should expect a health system to provide. Politically, there has been little room for considering the way the health system should be organised or the way doctors might be paid. The social environment is not seen as a health issue and the preventive and support services that might improve population health are a dead issue, discussed largely within small groups of experts. The evaluation of treatments is rarely discussed. And the major casualty is health itself.

CHAPTER 1

Irreconcilable interests

Every dollar of health care expenditure is, by accounting definition, a dollar of someone's income.

– Robert G. Evans, 1993

The way health care is financed largely determines how the benefits of the system are distributed between different groups. So when a nation chooses a health financing system, it is deciding who gets what, when and how.

Central to the politics of paying for health care are three groups with fundamentally different interests: providers (of services, technologies and therapies), consumers and government. Providers generally want economic and clinical autonomy and high incomes and profits. Consumers want affordable, timely access to quality, preferably prepaid, services. Given that over 70 per cent of health costs are paid for by the public purse in OECD countries, governments have a strong interest in the control of total health expenditures, especially in view of the propensity for health costs to increase faster than other prices.[1] Providers, of course, do not want cost control: restraining the resources devoted to health care limits, among other things, incomes and profits.

Where providers achieve their income and profit objectives, the cost to taxpayers and government budgets will be high. Depending on the financing system in place, it may also mean that consumers will face financial barriers to accessing services. On the other hand, in systems where governments are able to control health cost inflation, increases in provider incomes and profits can be contained. Where citizens are able to pre-pay fully for the costs of health care, either through tax or through public or private insurance, financial barriers to access will be eliminated – but without effective cost-control measures, the overall costs to the community will be inordinately high. In other words, a variety of health financing arrangements is possible, under which one or more of the key groups will get all, most or some of what they want. But no known system can fully satisfy the financial objectives of all three groups.

•

It is possible to imagine four separate "ideal" systems for paying for hospital and medical services: a free market, a national health service, private insurance, and public or national insurance. In practice, of course, most systems are admixtures of elements from several systems, but a dominant financing mechanism can be identified in each.

At one end of the spectrum is a **private market**, in which all practitioners are in private practice and are paid solely by patients. Providers are independent operators who choose their own fees and prices and set them at levels that the market will bear. Their incomes are not subsidised by the taxpayer. Clinicians choose the type of practice and its location. Consumers who cannot afford to pay fees may (or may not) receive services as charity cases. Hospitals are privately owned, for profit or not for profit, and are supported by fees. The whole system is financed by what, in present-day terms, are called user charges. In some instances, publicly subsidised hospital care may be available but patients will need to pay their doctors for the medical services they receive in hospitals – unless, again, they are cared for as charity cases. They will also pay fees for the use of the hospital. Because there is no agent, such as government, to bargain on behalf of consumers or to impose regulations, economic and clinical autonomy is preserved. Governments need not be concerned with the total cost to the community or with medical inflation rates (except in the highly unlikely case of a market system where citizens hold government responsible for outcomes). In any case, governments have very few levers through which expenditure control might be exercised in a private market system. The losing group here is consumers: charges mean that large numbers of people are denied access to care because of inability to pay. Geographical access will be a problem as well, because most doctors will choose to locate their practices in the well-off areas of major cities. Typically, curative services will dominate; prevention, rehabilitation and caring services will be scarce. A free-market system is likely to be stable until someone or some group begins to demand reform so that the not so well-off can access the system.

At the other end of the spectrum is a **national health service.** Under such a system, hospital and medical services are publicly financed and publicly provided. Doctors are generally not in private practice. Rather, they are remunerated on a salaried or contract basis. The whole population is covered for what are regarded as "medically necessary" medical and hospital services, with no charge (or low charges) at the point of service. Funds are collected through the tax system. The systems most closely fitting this model, at present, are that of Cuba and, in the OECD, Sweden, Greece, Italy and the United Kingdom.[2] In national health systems, governments have a high level of expenditure control. Consumers, for their part, do not face financial barriers to access and the system is simple: there are no bills, no insurance premiums, no gaps, no rebates, no safety nets and no complicated schedules of benefits to understand. Providers, however, do not get what they want: they lose economic autonomy and are required to negotiate with governments over income and profit levels. But once a settlement is reached with providers and the system is established, the tendency is towards stability, as actors work within the parameters that have been negotiated.

In the third type of system, **private insurance** is the dominant financing method. In this case, citizens or their employers prepay for health care through private insurance companies. Clinicians are in private practice, hospitals are (typically) private and providers – including insurance agencies – enjoy high levels of economic and professional autonomy. Government's role is restricted to regulation and there is no bargaining with providers over price, practice location and the like. Nor are governments concerned about levels of health expenditure, except where they have assumed a level of responsibility for the poor or where they provide tax subsidies for the costs of insurance premiums. In fact, a pure private health insurance system without taxpayer subsidies and public regulation is not possible in the modern world.[3] In practice, private financing systems are heavily subsidised by taxpayers, especially to protect those who cannot afford to pay. If they were not, there would be far fewer doctors, nurses and hospitals and far fewer medical procedures and technologies. Doctors would be eking out a meagre living, just as George Bernard Shaw described them as doing in England around the turn of the twentieth century, before the advent of public subsidy.

In this scenario, markets rather than governments determine total health spending. Providers get most of what they want from private insurance arrangements and governments are not directly affected by the operation of the system. Consumers, however, lose out. A proportion, usually upwards of 15 per cent in industrialised countries, cannot afford private insurance premiums and so have no protection against the costs of hospital and medical services. Another large group is unable to afford comprehensive cover and is thus under-insured. User charges may be high, even for the insured.

Private insurance systems have another major drawback. Total health expenditure is likely to be inordinately high, which increases the cost of insurance, making it more difficult for low and even middle income earners to afford cover. There are a number of reasons for high costs. Because private insurance systems are reimbursement systems – patients are reimbursed retrospectively for whatever expenses they incur – there is little incentive for providers or consumers to limit either the cost or the volume of services. Of course, insurance agencies will wish to control costs. But they will be unable to do so because of the fragmentation of the industry and the multiple independent providers with which they must do business. As the health finance specialist Gerard Anderson and his colleagues describe the United States, "money flows from households to the providers of health care through a vast network of relatively uncoordinated pipes and capillaries of various sizes."[4] The incentives induce payers, who are interested only in their own costs, to shift those costs to other payers – as, for example, when insurers require patients to pay higher user charges. Such systems are usually called "multi-payer" systems (discussed further in chapter five) in contrast to "single payer" systems, in which a single agency, such as a government or a health insurance commission, has both the incentive and the capacity to control total expenditures. Administrative costs are high owing to the multiple agencies and transactions involved.

The system that conforms most closely to this model today is that of the United States, where public funding as a percentage of total health expenditure is the lowest in the OECD but health spending is the highest. The country with the second lowest share of public financing, excluding the low-income countries of Mexico and Korea, is Switzerland, where total health spending, at 11.1 per cent of GDP, is the second-highest in the OECD.[5]

Public health insurance is the fourth of the possible payment systems and the one that operates in most European countries and in Canada. Public, or national, health insurance differs from a national health service because the delivery system is not under public control. Physicians and other health professionals are usually in private practice rather than being salaried employees. Financing is generally through insurance contributions rather than from general taxation but, either way, public control of financing is integral. In practice, a variety of other payment mechanisms, such as private insurance and user charges, may operate alongside a public insurance system. Private payments may cover items like dental services or pharmaceuticals, which may not be included in the public plan, or they may finance alternatives to publicly provided services, such as private hospital insurance. Similarly, doctors may be paid in a variety of ways, including fee-for-service, contract and salary. As in national health services, government is the dominant or sole payer and can exercise a high level of control over total expenditures. Government can also largely determine the shape and size of the nation's health infrastructure, including the number of acute-care hospital beds, the number of doctors and so on. It is also able to negotiate with providers over price and volume of services and other crucial issues, such as the geographical location of practices and general health infrastructure. Under public health insurance, financial barriers to access are (normally) eliminated or kept low. Governments and consumers achieve their objectives but the economic autonomy of providers is usually restricted.

The operation of a market sector alongside the public sector in either a national health or a national health insurance system can change the rewards that accrue to the different parties. If governments are successful in restraining health cost inflation, providers may be able to move some of their activities to the private sector where there are fewer cost controls and a greater prospect of revenue from user charges, thereby increasing incomes and profits. However, total health care costs will be increased and citizens using private services will have to pay for them. The result is a two-tiered system, where only the relatively well-off have the choice of using privately financed services. The exodus of health professionals from the public system may mean longer waiting times in that sector and may also create a situation where governments have to offer higher remuneration to attract staff. A large private sector, however, is unlikely to develop where high quality, timely public sector services are available.

•

Where does Australia fit into this array of health financing systems? Medicare is a national health insurance system, offering the dual prospect of universal access and public control of expenditures. The expenditure control potential is reflected in figures for the period 1991 to 1999, which show that health spending in Australia increased only slightly faster than GDP.[6] Expenditure control is not popular with providers, however, because limiting the total amount of money in the health care system constrains incomes and profits. It is under conditions of expenditure control that agitation for privatisation often emerges because user charges and private health insurance can increase the total funds circulating in the health system.

For consumers, the benefits of public financing have not been fully realised in Australia. Public hospital services are prepaid under Medicare but governments have not used their powers to eliminate user charges for medical services. One reason for government inaction is that the Australian constitution prohibits "any form of civil conscription" of doctors and dentists. But the main reason seems to be the absence of sufficient political will to confront a powerful medical establishment. There is no way of knowing how the High Court would view a proposal to control medical fees by, for example, restricting Medicare rebates to doctors who do not charge fees. But an analysis of the two High Court decisions made in relation to this provision suggests that imposing limits on fees may not be interpreted as "civil conscription" because medical practitioners would be under no obligation to provide the services and could, if they chose, offer their services in the unsubsidised private market.[7]

Irrespective of whether public or private insurance is in operation, the freedom of Australian medical practitioners to set their own fees creates a dilemma that has existed since the Commonwealth began to subsidise medical costs in 1953. The controversies about user charges and the decline of bulk billing during 2003 are the same, in essence, as controversies which began in the 1950s. Under the private insurance system, introduced in 1953, the Commonwealth paid a subsidy through the private health insurance funds. The idea was that the insurance component should be approximately one third of the fee, that the Commonwealth benefit should constitute roughly another third and that user charges should make up the rest. As fee levels increased, however, the value of the Commonwealth share fell. Patients were left with a larger proportion to pay from their own pockets, particularly for surgical services. Even after the Commonwealth increased its benefits in 1960 patients were no better off – doctors simply raised their fees.[8]

Controversies over user charges and fees continued throughout the 1960s, culminating in the introduction, by the Gorton government in 1969, of a scheme that aimed to limit user charges to $5 for any one service. To succeed, the plan required that medical practitioners adhere to a schedule of fees based on the "most common fee," but – short of risking legal action in relation to the civil conscription clause – the government could not enforce the schedule. When asked what would happen if doctors chose not to adhere to the schedule, Prime Minister Gorton gave what has been called his "famous clarification":

> The AMA agrees with us, or I believe will agree with us, that its policy, and it will be its policy, to inform patients who ask what the common fee is, and what their own fee is, so that a patient will know whether he is going to be operated on, if that's what it is, on the basis of common fee or not.[9]

The situation is just as uncertain in 2004. For out-of-hospital medical services that are not bulk billed, Medicare pays a benefit of 85 per cent of the schedule fee. The size of the user charge depends on the fee the doctor chooses. Governments do not know whether increases in schedule fee levels will be passed on to consumers or whether they will be absorbed in higher medical fees.

Private financing – in the form of private insurance, user charges and full-cost payments – is a significant element of total Australian health financing, adding up to 31.6 per cent of the total in 2001–02.[10] Because it is the public financing sector that gives governments leverage over expenditure, it follows that the larger the role of public insurance, the more effectively governments will be able to restrain spending. Public financing is also more equitable because taxation is levied on the basis of income. Under the Howard government, however, the role of private insurance has been deliberately increased – as has been the contribution of private financing through user charges. Governments thus have less capacity than previously to control total costs and citizens are increasingly vulnerable to the impact of flat-rate user charges. The system is made unnecessarily complex by such features as safety nets, levy surcharges, tax rebates and front-end deductibles.

•

Different kinds of health financing systems result in different winners and losers. In systems dominated by markets and private finance, producers normally enjoy high levels of control over their incomes, profits, type of medical practice, practice location and so on. Consequently, large numbers of citizens encounter financial barriers, made worse by high levels of medical inflation, and are disadvantaged by the concentration of services in cities. In systems dominated by public finance, governments have the capacity to control health care costs and are able (but not always willing) to ensure that citizens can afford hospital and medical services. The outcomes of publicly and privately financed systems are therefore fundamentally different for different groups.

Australia's Medicare-based system is a very uneasy compromise, which affects how benefits are directed to one group or another. Consumers have access to prepaid (but not necessarily timely) hospital care but they face significant user charges for medical services. Providers have partial economic autonomy. The operation of a large private sector enhances incomes and profits and clinicians are free to set their own fees, although the existence of government fee schedules does exert downward pressure. Fee levels are also constrained by bulk billing, which intensifies competition where doctors are concentrated. The Commonwealth has a high level of control over its own expenditure through Medicare but its control of total health expenditure is weakened by the growth of the private sector, where it has much less influence, and by declining bulk-billing rates. A precarious balance exists between the main health players at any given moment. Any increase in the benefits flowing to one group will be to the detriment of another. The stage is set for perpetual struggle.

CHAPTER 2

Irreconcilable ideologies

Labor's Medicare... is a giant step towards the nationalisation of health care in Australia. If allowed to continue it will create a government monopoly in health, where patients will have no choice, doctors and nurses and other health care workers will be demoralised, and quality will decline.

– LIBERAL PARTY OF AUSTRALIA AND NATIONAL PARTY OF AUSTRALIA, 1984

The conflict between competing interests in health policy is a struggle over "ends" rather than "means." Policy-makers, interest groups, economists and researchers argue about whether health care should be seen as a product to be bought and sold in the marketplace like any other, or whether it should be seen as what economists call a "merit good." A "merit good" is regarded as so important to life that the free market must be overridden. According to this view, the community – through its government – provides health care for itself. Rather than relying on market outcomes, the system is financed and managed through publicly controlled institutions. Access to services is universal and a single criterion, "medical need," is used to set priorities. The question is whether health care, a multibillion-dollar industry, is an appropriate area for private practice, private for-profit activity and high incomes or whether there should be a level of community control over who gets what health services, when and how.

An additional dynamic intensifies Australian health policy disagreements. Unlike most OECD countries, Australia's political interests have never reached a "settlement" in relation to health. One of the main reasons is that the two major political parties take a radically different view of the appropriate "ends" of policy. The Labor Party has supported a large public sector and extensive public intervention for over a century while the Coalition parties have consistently supported a predominantly private system.

These positions reflect the contrasting ideological perspectives of the major parties. The Liberal and National parties are committed to a *residual* view of welfare, with citizens taking care of their own welfare needs through the family and the market, a position consistent with the ideology of individual responsibility and free enterprise. According to this view, government's role is limited to providing safety nets and emergency relief. Labor, by contrast, takes an *institutional* approach, based on the premise that many citizens are unable to provide for themselves in modern, industrialised societies. Poverty is seen as a product of economic and social systems rather than a result of individual failing, so the needs and predicaments of citizens are a legitimate area of public concern and social provision is one of the primary functions of the state. Both national health services and national health insurance schemes embody these latter values.

The competition between Labor and the Coalition has a long history in health policy. The Labor leader, John Curtin, told the federal parliament in 1938 that "national health services should be treated, in principle, in the same way as education. They should be free to all members of the community." In contrast, the Liberal Party leader, Robert Menzies, warned in 1944 that "non-contributory community benevolence" should not be allowed to replace "individual effort" and "individual contribution" and, further, that the taxation levels necessary to maintain social programs would deal a "fatal blow" to private enterprise.[1] The parties remain divided to the present day, although the Coalition's decision to retain elements of Medicare and Labor's support for direct public subsidies for private health insurance suggests a shift in the historical position.

The ideological persuasions of the Coalition and of the main medical unions are in natural harmony. The AMA, the Royal Australian College of General Practitioners, Private Doctors of Australia, the Association of Procedural Specialists and most other leading medical associations oppose government intervention, except to finance services for those who cannot afford to pay fees. As Thelma Hunter documented many years ago, the AMA believed that public intervention, in the form of a national insurance system or a salaried service, is "utterly inconsistent with the individualistic principles of private medical practice."[2] On the other side of the divide, public opinion polls demonstrate that a majority of Australian consumers have supported Labor's policies and proposals since 1943.[3]

•

The historical "strife of interests" in Australia has hinged almost entirely on a single issue: whether health will be funded predominantly from public or private sources. For more than a century, organised medicine vehemently resisted any policy or institution with the potential to reduce the size of the private market. Health politics around the turn of the twentieth century was dominated by campaigns against what the profession termed "hospital abuse," the admission of people "who could afford to pay private fees" to public hospitals. Doctors wanted admission restricted to the indigent so that all other citizens would be forced to purchase services in the private market. The profession also opposed any form of payment by government. This included the capitation system, under which doctors are paid "per capita" for persons on their lists rather than "per service," as in a fee-for-service system. They also opposed all forms of public health insurance. The British Medical Association in Australia, as the AMA was known until 1962, told the Royal Commission on National Insurance in 1923 that "no existing form of national health insurance would be acceptable."[4]

Conflict erupted every time governments – mainly Labor – tried to take control of public hospitals and open them to all citizens, as was attempted in New South Wales between 1910 and 1916, in Tasmania between 1912 and 1918 and at various times in Queensland during the long period of Labor office from 1915 to 1957. The medical profession also vehemently opposed the introduction of any services, such as infant welfare services, school health services, tuberculosis and venereal disease clinics and bush nursing services, which were to be publicly funded and provided by salaried staff.[5]

Conflict erupted, too, when Coalition governments at the Commonwealth level proposed to introduce national social insurance, along European lines, financed by citizen and employer contributions rather than predominantly from taxation, as in the 1920s and 1930s. Coalition governments believed it had been a mistake to finance pensions from taxation and that unless something were done, in the words of one Liberal minister, "the whole financial fabric of the Commonwealth" would collapse.[6] The expert brought from England to design a national scheme, Sir Walter Kinnear, insisted that pensions and health "be treated as one organic whole."[7] The subsequent opposition of the medical profession was the main reason that the 1938 legislation, which passed both houses of parliament, was finally abandoned.[8]

While differences between the major parties over hospitals and directly provided services were apparent from the earliest days, the policy position polarised dramatically in the 1940s. Since that time, Labor proposals have been strenuously opposed by the medical profession and, more recently, by private hospitals and private health insurance funds. Coalition policies, on the other hand, have generally found support among these groups.

A national health service, involving a pharmaceutical benefits scheme, a national medical scheme and a prepaid hospital scheme, open to all citizens, was proposed by Labor in the 1940s. Medical opposition, involving years of negotiations, two High Court cases and a constitutional amendment, prevented all but the hospital scheme from coming into operation.

After regaining office in 1949, the Coalition introduced its own national health system, a publicly subsidised private-insurance scheme. The policy had been developed not by the government but by the medical profession, in response to Labor's nationalisation proposals. The national hospital system was abolished in order to induce, if not force, people to buy "voluntary" insurance. A pensioner medical service covered general practitioner services but did not include access to specialists. The uninsured were excluded from public subsidy, which was available only through private insurance.

When Labor returned to government in the 1970s, a national health insurance scheme was put in place, amid a storm of opposition from Coalition and private sector interests. Included in the policy was an almost identical version of the hospital scheme of the 1940s. Medibank, as the program was known, began operating in 1975 but was abolished in stages by the incoming Fraser Coalition government. The voluntary health insurance system of the 1950s and 1960s was reinstated in 1981. After Labor's return to power in 1983, national health insurance – including Australia's third system of prepaid hospital care – was introduced once again. Like previous Labor policies, the new scheme, Medicare, met with strong opposition from the Coalition parties and private sector interests and gave rise to an eighteen-month strike by procedural specialists in New South Wales. Medicare was nevertheless introduced successfully. Its main features are listed below.

Despite increasing public support for the new scheme, the Coalition was slow to alter its established policy position. In 1987, with an

---

Medicare: the main features

Universal insurance for medical services, out of hospital. The benefit rate is 85 per cent of the schedule fee. If the doctor charges above the schedule fee, the difference, or "gap," is paid by the patient. Private insurance for out-of-hospital medical services is not permitted.

Universal insurance for medical services, in hospital. There is no charge for medical services to public patients in public hospitals (doctors are paid by hospitals on a salaried or sessional basis). A Medicare benefit of 75 per cent of the schedule fee is paid for medical services for private patients in hospital. In this case, private insurance funds top up the benefit to 100 per cent of the schedule fee and, since 2000, meet other fees above the schedule, under certain circumstances.

Prepaid treatment in public hospitals for public patients. Private insurance for private accommodation in both public and private hospitals is available.

An optional system of bulk billing, through which doctors send the bill to the Health Insurance Commission, rather than charging the patient. In this case, the doctor accepts 85 per cent of the schedule fee as full payment for the service.

The principle of contribution according to ability to pay. The scheme is partly financed by a Medicare levy of 1.5 per cent of taxable income, which supplements financing from general taxation.

---

election looming, public support for Medicare stood at 64 per cent with only 15 per cent of people favouring abolition. Ignoring opinion polls, the Coalition campaigned on a policy of replacing Medicare with a predominantly private system. "The Medicare system is a total disaster," the party leader, John Howard, told radio 2GB on 1 June 1987. "We'll pull it right apart... the second thing we will do is get rid of bulk billing." The Coalition lost the election but continued to oppose Medicare up to and beyond the *Fightback!* policy prepared for the 1993 election. Support for a predominantly private system was stated clearly in the *Fightback!* proposals:

> Over time the Coalition will reduce the dominance of government in the nation's health... There is a myth among many health professionals that only governments can provide services of such fundamental importance to public welfare as health. Yet the experience of recent years has shown that the dead hand of public sector management leads in the end to deterioration of service to the public and to the demoralisation of the professionals and other workers in the system.[9]

The policy specified in some detail the way that the private sector would be progressively expanded to "restore the viability of private medical practice and private health insurance." The *Fightback!* health policy was a major feature of the Coalition's campaign for the 1993 election but proved to be very costly in terms of votes. The shadow health minister lost his seat and research shows that had each party attracted equal support on health, the Coalition would have won the election.[10]

Popular support for Medicare and the prospect of further electoral defeat appear to have induced the Coalition parties to adopt their present "preserve Medicare" position. Community support for the system rose steadily from 64 per cent in 1987 to 93 per cent in 1996–97.[11] A Liberal Party MP and former president of the AMA, Dr Brendan Nelson, acknowledged that "market solutions" for health were rejected by the electorate in 1993.[12] He has also attested to the impact of community views on party policy for the 1996 election:

> Opinion polls conducted prior to the last federal election indicated overwhelming support by Australians for Medicare and the universal

> access to public health services that this entails. And if you want to touch a broad nerve in public opinion polling then any politician just has to suggest some sort of change to universal and/or so-called free access to health care.[13]

In 1996, continued opposition to Medicare may have cost the Coalition parties another election. Unlike previous Labor programs, Medicare had operated long enough to become "established" in the Australian context. The prepaid hospital scheme of the 1940s was in place for only six years and Medibank operated for only a few months before government changed hands. Medicare, in contrast, had operated for twelve years when the Howard government came to office.

•

That the Coalition committed itself reluctantly to maintaining Medicare "in its entirety" is apparent in the privatisation policies it has pursued and in negative sentiments expressed by the prime minister since gaining office. It should be said here, however, that the role that private insurance is expected to play under a national health insurance scheme has never been fully clarified by either major party. So it is unclear exactly what "retaining Medicare" means or even what is meant by retaining Medicare "in its entirety." A large public hospital sector has existed in Australia since the first half of the nineteenth century and was an integral element of previous private health insurance systems. A significant private sector of hospital and medical services has existed since the introduction of national insurance in the 1970s.

The Fraser Coalition government promised to maintain Medibank and, despite a step-by-step dismantling process, always insisted that it had done so, until the last vestiges of universality were finally abolished in 1981. For that government, Medibank meant an element of universality, no matter how small and no matter how large the user charges. In office from 1983 to 1996, Labor championed national health insurance and a strong public hospital sector, leaving the private sector to operate as a supplementary system without public subsidy after 1986. During that time, the number of people holding private insurance steadily declined from 50 per cent in June 1984 just after Medicare was introduced, to 33.6 per cent when Labor lost office and by a further 2.9 per cent in the early Howard years.

The differences that remain between the major parties have been described by Brendan Nelson in the following terms:

> The previous government's policy position was mostly to say that private health insurance and the private health sector was supplementary to Medicare. Labor thought it had a role but in their view a relatively minor role compared with Medicare – and a role which would phase out over time. This government, however, holds a view that we need a robust and healthy private health financing sector... the government's message is loud and clear: that the private sector is a vital component of the long-term viability of Medicare and the public hospital system.[14]

In line with this position, the Commonwealth–State Health Care Agreements, which covered public hospital funding for the five-year period from 1998 onwards, specified that one of the policy objectives was "to recognise and support the significant role that the private sector plays in the provision of health services in Australia and the right of Australians to choose private health care."[15] In the Australian context, then, maintaining Medicare "in its entirety" may take a variety of forms. In the first two terms of the Howard government, it included substantial privatisation.

CHAPTER 3

Irreconcilable claims

[I]f you ever hear Howard proposing to means-test entry to public hospitals you'll know he's finally reached the last item on his twenty-year-old agenda to roll back Medicare.

– Ross Gittens, 2003

Since assuming office, the Howard government has gradually but steadily moved health policy in the direction of privatisation, following very closely the strategy mapped out in Liberal and National Party policy statements between 1984 and 1993. The changes have reduced access to medical, diagnostic and a range of ancillary services by increasing financial barriers. New funding has been used to expand private insurance rather than increase Medicare services, with obvious implications for timely access to hospital procedures for "Medicare only" citizens.

One of the Howard government's first decisions was to abolish the Commonwealth Dental Program in January 1997, despite the fact that a health department review had shown that the scheme provided services for 500,000 low-income people annually and had significantly improved dental health. Funding for family planning services was cut by 10 per cent in the first year of office. The 1996 budget reduced the disability accommodation budget by $80 million and increased user charges for hearing services, for Home and Community Care Program services and, by 20 per cent, for medicines. Family Allowance Supplement recipients were no longer entitled to Health Care Cards unless they were in receipt of the full supplement. A year later, the 1997 budget restricted the range of medications available at a concessional rate to low-income earners and increased the waiting time for a Health Care Card, available only to very low-income earners, from four to eight weeks. Forty-three Medicare offices in metropolitan and urban areas were closed in 1997–98.[1] All of these changes had the greatest impact on low-income earners, a majority of whom are women. Women comprise 65 per cent of age pensioners, for example, and 93 per cent of sole parent beneficiaries. Significantly, changes at the very beginning of the term of office broke a key Coalition election promise to preserve all Commonwealth pensioner concessions.

At the same time as selected services were being wound back and user charges increased, new expenditure was set aside to underpin the private sector. A $2 million publicity campaign to promote private insurance was launched in 1996 and was followed by the reintroduction of a public subsidy for private insurance. The Private Health Insurance Incentives Scheme, introduced on 1 July 1997, incorporated a "carrot and stick" approach to consumer behaviour. Under the "carrot" part of the scheme, single people earning up to $35,000 per year and couples earning up to $70,000 became eligible for subsidies of $125 and $250 respectively if they held private insurance. Families with one child earning up to $70,000 became eligible for a subsidy of $450, the income threshold increasing by $3000 for each additional child. Under the "stick" part of the scheme, high-income earners (singles earning more than $50,000, families earning more than $100,000) were required to pay a Medicare levy surcharge of 1 per cent of income if they did not hold private insurance.[2] These measures were intended to stop the rate of decline in private insurance and – according to the government – "hopefully achieve some increase," perhaps up to a level of 40 per cent of coverage.[3] The cost to the Commonwealth was $600 million a year or 11.5 per cent of Commonwealth expenditure on public hospitals.[4]

The hoped-for increase did not eventuate. Most high-income people already had private health insurance and, for those on low incomes, the financial incentive was weak. The measures did nothing to reduce the co-payments paid by the privately insured. The cost of private insurance premiums continued to rise and, as costs rose, the proportion of people privately insured continued to fall. The rate of decline was slightly lower than in 1996–97 but the same as in 1995–96. Between June 1995 and June 1996, private insurance coverage fell by 1.3 per cent and then, during the next twelve months, by a further 1.7 per cent. Between June 1997 and June 1998, the first year of the operation of the incentives scheme, coverage fell by a further 1.3 per cent to 30.6 per cent.[5]

As it became clear that the scheme was not increasing private insurance levels, the AMA began to call for further reform. In February 1998, the association's federal president called for the reintroduction of means testing for access to public hospitals, a policy which the profession had developed more than a century before. The prime minister is reported to have agreed that further reforms were needed. By May, the AMA was publicly branding the Private Health Insurance Incentives Scheme a "disaster." Relations with the health minister, Dr Michael Wooldridge, were described by the AMA as "absolutely appalling." The organisation announced that henceforth it would deal directly with the prime minister because Mr Howard had "shown an interest" in resolving the health insurance issue "with an election ahead."[6]

•

The policy for the 1998 election was announced as part of the government's wide-ranging proposal for a GST – a goods and services tax. The prime minister promised a large increase in the public subsidy for private insurance, in the form of a rebate of 30 per cent of the cost of health insurance contributions. The initial cost to taxpayers was $1.6 billion dollars per annum but this sum rose quickly as further incentives promoted private coverage. Significantly, the rebate is not means tested, providing a large windfall gain – paid for by general taxpayers – for many well-off people who already held private insurance. Enabling legislation was introduced into parliament on 11 November and was passed by the Senate on 10 December. The scheme began operating on 1 January 1999.

Despite its cost, the 30 per cent rebate brought only a small increase in the number of people buying private insurance. In its first nine months, private insurance coverage rose by less than 1 per cent, from 30.1 per cent to 30.9 per cent. The subsidy did slow the steady decline that had become a feature of the system but, after fifteen months, only 32.2 per cent of the population was covered. Clearly, further measures were needed to promote the private sector.

In the May 1999 budget it was announced that the principle of community rating would be modified. Since public subsidies for private health insurance were introduced in the early 1950s, pure community rating had been mandatory in Australia. Insurers had not been allowed to refuse to insure people or to vary the price of premiums on grounds such as age, sex, health status, service use, employment or occupation. Now, under Lifetime Health Cover, as the initiative is called, private insurers were to set different premium rates for different people, depending on the age at which the person first became privately insured. For all persons over 30 years of age, except those born on or before 1 July 1934 (that is, they were over 65 when the new system was introduced), private health insurance premiums increased by 2 per cent for each year of non-membership, up to a maximum of 70 per cent.

In an aggressive marketing campaign, the government described Lifetime Health Cover as "part of a comprehensive strategy" to arrest the decline in private insurance coverage, "to strike a better balance between public and private sectors" and to ensure that citizens have a "level of choice as well as universal access to excellent health care."[7] The scheme was intended to combat two groups who were allegedly undermining the old rules: "hit and run" members, who became privately insured for certain elective procedures but later dropped their insurance, and young, healthy people who did not buy private insurance or dropped their private cover when premiums rose, leaving a greater proportion of older and less healthy people in the private insurance pool.

Arrangements for Lifetime Health Cover were announced and publicised twelve months before they were to take effect. Anyone of any age who bought private insurance before 1 July 2000 was able to avoid the age excess. The government launched an $8.7 million publicity campaign to induce people to "Run for Cover." In response, an additional 2.08 million people, 11 per cent of the population, entered the private insurance system in the three months before the deadline. When the government extended the deadline by two weeks, another 550,000 people joined up.[8] By September 2000, 45.8 per cent of the population were privately insured, an increase of 50 per cent in the 21 months after the rebate began.

The success of the Lifetime Health Cover campaign appears to have been almost entirely due to the fear created by the government that access to public hospitals would be restricted. The extensively broadcast "Run for Cover" message, echoed by health care providers, created uncertainty and an impression that Medicare was in crisis. The health economist, Jim Butler, has examined the series of rebates introduced by the Howard government. He found that the rebate schemes had almost no effect, probably giving rise to an increased coverage of around 2 per cent. According to Butler's analysis, almost all of the 50 per cent increase in private health insurance membership was due to Lifetime Health Cover.[9]

Work by the health economist, John Deeble, corroborates this position. He points out that the responsiveness of private insurance to price ("price elasticity") is low and that it was both "predicted and predictable" that the rebate would not substantially change private insurance take-up rates. He argues that if the 30 per cent rebate had had little effect, then it must follow that the prospect of small increases in premium prices, years hence, could not have had a significant impact either. His conclusion is that "the only plausible explanation" for the 50 per cent increase in private health insurance coverage "is that it was the 'fear factor' which dominated."[10]

To further bolster the attractiveness of private insurance, the government reintroduced gap insurance for in-hospital medical services in August 2000. A "gap" is the difference between the insurance benefit and the fee charged by a doctor, variously called a user charge, an out-of-pocket expense, a patient co-payment or patient cost sharing. These expenses were thought to deter people from taking out private insurance.

Controversy over "gaps" is as old as public subsidies for private insurance in Australia. The medical profession has always insisted that the insurance benefit should not cover the full fee, ostensibly "to protect the doctor from frivolous demands by patients"![11] But organised medicine feared that once governments and health funds paid the full fee, pressure would mount for fees to be standardised. As we've seen, the size of the co-payments first became a vexed political issue under voluntary insurance in the 1950s and 1960s when, after the Commonwealth increased its subsidy, doctors raised their fees, leaving out-of-pocket expenses as high as ever. Governments are no better placed to control the size of co-payments under national health insurance.

Medical gap insurance was originally prohibited for all Medicare services, in the belief that the co-payments would deter steep rises in medical fees. Lifting this prohibition became one of the key demands of the AMA and the procedural specialists. As part of the settlement of the 1984–85 NSW doctors' strike, modified gap insurance was introduced, permitting coverage of the difference between the Medicare benefit (which was 75 per cent of the schedule fee) and the schedule fee for in-hospital medical services. Private insurance for out-of-hospital medical services was still prohibited.

Throughout the 1990s, controversy raged over the size of gaps, with private sector interests arguing for the introduction of full-gap insurance. The Labor government finally introduced legislation in 1995, allowing health funds to offer insurance for the gap between the schedule fee and the doctor's fee for in-hospital medical services, in cases where insurance funds were able to negotiate contracts with doctors and private hospitals to provide services at specified prices. A few private hospitals and a handful of individual doctors came into the scheme but, overall, the legislation had little impact on the gaps that existed. The AMA and the Association of Procedural Specialists continued to fight strongly against the notion of contracts. The Howard government attempted to introduce legislation in 1998 for, among other things, gap insurance, on condition that there be agreements between insurance funds and doctors that would ensure that there would be either "no gaps" or "known gaps." The gap insurance provisions of the legislation were withdrawn in February 1999, reportedly in response to opposition from surgeons. Negotiations between the government and the AMA continued but the situation gave rise to intense conflict between moderates and radicals within organised medicine. Eventually, a vote of no confidence was passed in the AMA leadership at an extraordinary general meeting in 1999.[12]

Full gap insurance was finally reintroduced for in-hospital medical services in August 2000. The *Health Legislation Amendment (Gap Cover Schemes) Act 2000* contains no requirement that there be a contract between insurance funds and doctors, but the health minister must approve all schemes before they begin. Schemes must not have an inflationary impact on premiums or doctors' fees and must genuinely deliver "no or known gaps." Doctors participating must inform patients in writing of the amount they must pay and should disclose any financial interests they have in recommending products or services to patients. To protect the clinical autonomy of doctors and to prevent the development of US-style "managed care" arrangements, Regulation 3C(4)(h) of the *National Health Regulations 1954* provides that:

> The scheme must provide for the maintenance of the professional freedom of medical practitioners, within the scope of accepted clinical practice, to identify appropriate treatments when providing professional attention to a person or persons insured under a no gap or a known gap policy.

The proportion of in-hospital medical services for which there was no gap increased from 60 per cent of all services in September 2000 to 81 per cent in March 2003, in the first two-and-a-half years of operation. However, the Private Health Insurance Administration Council, which is responsible for monitoring the scheme, warns that the figures should be treated with caution because of changes in reporting systems.[13]

Clearly, privately insured hospital patients benefit from these arrangements, but at the cost of higher premiums. John Deeble has shown that medical gap benefits more than doubled between 1998–99 and 2001–02, from $253 million to $598 million, during which time the number of medical services grew by only 38 per cent.[14] There was a startling increase in the level of medical benefits paid above the schedule fee. In 1998–99, above–schedule fee benefits were $12.2 million, but by 2000–01 these had risen more than tenfold to $126.8 million. In the following year they increased again, this time by almost double, to $247.8 million. These payments represent a significant income transfer to physicians. According to Garry Richardson, the Private Health Insurance Administration Council commissioner, this trend is expected to continue as private health insurance organisations compete with each other to improve the attractiveness of their products. He notes, however, that these developments result in "increased costs for the registered organisations and will translate into pressure on contribution rates."[15] In other words, the reintroduction of full gap insurance for in-hospital medical services has removed moderating pressure on medical fees. Patient co-payments above the schedule fee are now reimbursed by private insurance funds, increasing the cost of health care for the community as a whole and increasing the cost to general taxpayers who meet 30 per cent of the cost of private health insurance premiums.

CHAPTER 4

The bulk-billing impasse: fifty years of fighting over fees

The public may be excused for thinking that the Federal Government's medical benefits scheme was aimed at helping them meet the high cost of sickness. The medical profession clearly sees it in another light. To them it's a doctors' benefit scheme.

– *SYDNEY MORNING HERALD* EDITORIAL, 12 MARCH 1970

Because user charges deter people from seeking medical care, bulk billing is a foundational building block of Medicare. It is the mechanism through which the full cost of out-of-hospital medical services are paid for from taxation, without a charge to the patient at the point of service. Yet, in the same year that privately insured citizens began to enjoy the benefits of the extension of gap insurance, citizens relying on Medicare began to face higher out-of-pocket payments because of a decline in the number of doctors willing to bulk bill. The change has serious implications for access and equity.

After 1984, the incidence of bulk billing steadily increased, reaching a peak of 72.3 per cent of all services in 1999–2000. After this point, however, rates began to decline steadily and by December 2003 had fallen to 66.6 per cent. Bulk-billing rates for general practitioner services peaked at 81 per cent in 1996–97 but had fallen to 66.5 per cent by December 2003. As we've seen, the decline sparked a storm of controversy and, in 2002, became a major political issue. Alarm intensified when the prime minister announced in March 2003 that bulk billing was never meant to be universal. Mr Howard told parliament that he supported universality but that this did not mean that each and every service would be bulk billed. Along with the treasurer, Peter Costello, he argued that bulk billing should be focused primarily, if not exclusively, on low-income earners. Both men vehemently and misleadingly denied that their approach constituted the introduction of a means test, despite the fact that low-income earners cannot be identified without such a test.

Holding to his pro-Medicare rhetoric, the prime minister claimed that universality means "the entitlement of every Australian, irrespective of means, to the Medicare rebate," not "some sort of universal guarantee" to bulk billing.[1] Just as the previous Liberal prime minister, Malcolm Fraser, had claimed in the late 1970s that Medibank had been retained because a small element of universality remained, so Mr Howard reformulated the meaning of universality. In his interpretation, it means that so long as everyone is eligible for reimbursement from Medicare for the cost of a medical service it doesn't matter how small the proportion of the fee that the reimbursement covers. The position of consumers is similar to their position under private health insurance, prior to the introduction of Medicare: people going to a doctor are entitled to a public subsidy but they have no idea what proportion of the medical fee will be covered, nor the size of the co-payment that they will be asked to pay.

Amid increasing controversy, a 2003 survey of 1924 doctors across 24 health areas, funded by NSW Health, found that rates of bulk billing were falling rapidly. Just over 80 per cent of doctors interviewed cited inadequate Medicare payments as the main reason for the decline. The evidence gathered by the study suggested that in six months only 22 per cent of doctors would offer full bulk-billing services, with rates dropping to as low as 4 per cent in some country districts.[2] Another study found that the average patient co-payment had increased from $17.43 in June 2001 to $18.68 a year later.[3] For general practitioner consultations, the average co-payment was $12 but in some areas is said to be as high as $35.[4] Average co-payments increased at the rate of 7 per cent per annum in 2001–02.

The AMA maintains that the decline in bulk billing is due to a shortage of general practitioners and the government's failure to maintain the value of Medicare schedule fees, especially in view of increasing practice costs. Successive federal governments, according to the AMA president, Dr Kerryn Phelps, "failed to recognise the demise of Medicare." People were being asked to contribute more of their household incomes towards the cost of health care. Serious doctor shortages had developed because medicine was no longer an attractive career, she argued, and "our brightest and best students" pursue other training while government action means that "bulk billing has passed its use by date." Dr Phelps pronounced bulk billing "effectively dead," with no prospect of revival. Under the circumstances, policies had to be developed to ensure access for "the disadvantaged – the elderly, pensioners, unemployed, the chronically ill and low income families."[5]

For its part, the Commonwealth claimed that the main problem was the geographical maldistribution of doctors. The undersupply of practitioners in regional and remote areas is said to result in low levels of competition, reducing the financial incentive to bulk bill. Both points of view have validity. Certainly, bulk billing is considerably lower in regional and remote areas and in the Australian Capital Territory, which has the lowest supply of general practitioners in the country. But the issue of the value of the schedule fee is more complex. Schedule fees are indexed by a formula developed by the Department of Finance. Calculations showed that the rebate for a standard general practitioner consultation had kept pace with increases in the consumer price index but that the value of the rebate had fallen compared with average full-time weekly earnings. Deeble argues that in 1984 the Medicare rebate was deliberately set at a generous level to attract the support of the profession.[6] In the last decade, that margin of generosity has been extinguished. Calculating back in time using average full-time weekly earnings as a guide, the rebate for a standard general practitioner consultation in 1984–85 was the equivalent of $30.15. It roughly maintained that value until 1992–93, when it began to fall, reaching $25.03 in 2002–03.[7] On the basis of a relative value study conducted by the Department of Health and Ageing and the AMA in 2001–02, however, the AMA argued that the schedule fee for a standard general practitioner consultation should be increased by 100 per cent to $50.[8] In contrast, Deeble argued that an increase of $6 in the rebate, at a cost to the Commonwealth of approximately $500 million, would have returned incomes to 1984 levels.[9]

According to the Doctors Reform Society, a small group of pro-Medicare practitioners, the sources of doctor dissatisfaction are complex and diverse. In its submission to the Senate Select Committee on Medicare, the society argued that:

> Doctors are dissatisfied for a wide variety of reasons which include a relative decline in income due to a failure of rebate rises to keep pace with the cost of running a practice, increasing administrative and bureaucratic responsibilities, decreased availability of locums and after hours support, lack of Government support for medical indemnity issues and overwork in areas of GP undersupply.[10]

Bulk-billing rates are declining, according to the society, because practitioners are in a position to do something about their dissatisfaction: they are permitted to charge as much as they like. Health care is a seller's market and even if it creates hardship, patients will often find the necessary money.[11]

After more than a year of controversy and press speculation, the government announced its response, "A Fairer Medicare," in April 2003. It claimed that the policy package would "make Medicare fairer for all Australians, improve affordable access to GPs, reduce upfront fees for some patients, strengthen safety nets for families and concession cardholders and train more doctors."[12]

Doctors who agree to bulk bill Health Care Card holders ("participating doctors") would receive additional payments ranging from $1 per service in capital cities to $6.30 in small country towns. The Medicare rebate for non–concession cardholders would not be increased.

Upfront costs for non-cardholding patients of participating doctors were to fall. Doctors would be able to recover from the patient only the amount charged above the schedule fee and would bill Medicare direct for the rebate. (Previously, this was not allowed: doctors who bulk billed had not been allowed to charge a co-payment.) Under the new arrangements, the doctor would be paid within two days and patients would no longer have to find the full amount at the time of service, nor visit a Medicare office to claim the rebate. Doctors who did not participate would not be allowed to bill Medicare directly for the rebate. The patients of these doctors would continue to pay the full amount upfront at the time of service.

Private medical insurance, which Medicare replaced, was to have been introduced where out-of-hospital medical expenses (for specialists and general practitioners) exceeded $1000 per year.

There would be new safety net arrangements for cardholders who faced out-of-pocket expenses above $500 per annum. The government would reimburse 80 per cent of the cost of services in excess of that amount. Practices with high numbers of concession cardholders would receive additional payments of up to $20,000 per annum. An estimated 800 general practitioners in areas of doctor shortages would be assisted financially to employ nurses to alleviate pressure. And an additional 234 medical school places would be created in 2004.

The health minister, Kay Patterson, said these arrangements would preserve the core of Medicare and that "everyone will continue to have access to the Medicare rebate... As is the case now, doctors will be free to bulk bill whomever they choose." In relation to the reintroduction of private insurance for out-of-hospital medical services, she said that the changes "will give people a new choice in private insurance and peace of mind in knowing that they are covered against high out-of-hospital medical gap payments."[13] In other words, private medical insurance was to replace Medicare for part of the cost of medical services.

The government's response was strongly criticised by a wide range of welfare groups, by some groups of doctors and by all the other political parties, including Labor. It was claimed that the government was undermining the principle of universality on which Medicare is based and turning it into a scheme targeting welfare beneficiaries. Critics also claimed that the changes would hasten rather than stem the decline in bulk billing (which was arguably the government's real intention). The new arrangements, it was said, would legitimise co-payments and build them into the system. Since 1984, a general resistance to large gap payments had promoted bulk billing and restrained fee increases; the new system would encourage doctors to limit bulk billing to the target cardholder group and charge other patients what the market would bear.

The argument that the new arrangements would lead to further declines in bulk billing was challenged repeatedly by the prime minister, the health minister and, at the Senate inquiry, by Senator Susan Knowles. But critics all agreed that the trend would be accelerated. In the opinion of a member of the Doctors Reform Society, "economic disincentives to bulk billing anyone without a concession card are built into the proposal."[14]

Nor, according to the critics, did the package guarantee bulk billing for cardholders, who would have to rely on a safety net after they had spent $500 of their own. Experience in Australia with safety net schemes is that they are complex, not easily understood and that people fail to claim their entitlements. Under a scheme operating in the early 1970s, many qualified people failed to seek assistance, a situation likely to recur. Moreover, such schemes are administratively difficult and expensive. As John Deeble told the Senate Committee on Medicare, "safety nets are about the most inefficient, complicated, expensive and, in a sense, unmanageable way of handling those [co-payment] costs."[15]

Also under fierce attack was the proposal to reintroduce private out-of-hospital medical insurance, a measure the insurance industry has been promoting for years. The proposal would have further increased private financing through private insurance, rather than through Medicare. Private insurance was to have been allowed only for expenses in excess of $1000 per annum, so the measure would only benefit people with high health costs: few individuals, or even families, would incur out-of-pocket expenses of $1000 for general practitioner services. Medical inflation, however, would change that over time.

Legislation was introduced into parliament in May 2003 but ran into trouble in the Senate, where the government does not have a majority. On 15 May that chamber voted to establish a select committee to inquire into Medicare. Although the terms of reference did not include specialist services, the committee's brief was broad. It was asked to "inquire into and report on the access to and affordability of general practice under Medicare," with particular reference to a wide range of matters, including the impact of the current Medicare rebate on practitioner incomes and the viability of bulk billing, the impact of general practitioner shortages and the "likely impact on access, affordability and quality services for individuals, in the short and longer term" of the government's proposals. The committee was also asked to consider alternatives that could "improve the Medicare principles of access and affordability," particularly in relation to dental services, a possible reallocation of the private health insurance rebate and "alternative remuneration models that would satisfy medical practitioners but would not compromise the principle of universality which underlies Medicare."

Public hearings were held in major cities across the country. The committee's report, *Medicare – Health Care or Welfare?*, was presented in October. It found that out-of-pocket expenses for patients had risen "quite markedly." Among general practitioners, the committee found a "strongly held perception" that their incomes had fallen in relation to both specialists and other professionals but there was "no compelling evidence" that the cost of running a practice "had outgrown the CPI." The committee concluded that general practice remained financially viable but found that the real incomes of general practitioners who bulk billed *exclusively* had fallen relative to average weekly earnings.[16]

After examining alternatives that would improve access to primary care services, the committee recommended that the Commonwealth resume financing public dental services, extend allied health service programs and expand training for doctors and nurses. The focus of medical practice should shift "towards more integrated primary care," the committee concluded and, in this respect, fee-for-service private medical practice was "a roadblock to progress." It recommended that Medicare grants be used to establish community health centres in areas of need and establish bulk-billing clinics in or near public hospitals in areas where bulk billing is low. On the question of the rebate, the committee argued that there was insufficient evidence to make a definitive judgement but enough evidence to "cast doubt on [its] overall effectiveness." *Medicare – Health Care or Welfare?* recommended that an independent rebate enquiry be established.[17]

Nor did the committee accept the government's argument that the legislation would preserve universality. It criticised the proposal to reintroduce private medical insurance as a safety net and argued that the scheme would "trigger a fall in bulk billing" for those without concession cards and lead to inevitable problems at the margins of entitlement. It concluded that:

> The remedies for the current problems in Medicare do not lie in refocusing the system on concessional patients, nor in tinkering with the criteria for the granting of those concession cards, but rather in a reorientation towards the role of Medicare as a universal insurer, with equal benefits for everyone.[18]

With no prospect of the Fairer Medicare legislation passing through the Senate, the government – and its new health minister, Tony Abbott – set about developing a new policy package. The prime minister announced Medicare Plus on 18 November 2003. In addition to the $917 million proposed under the previous scheme, the new package added an extra $1.5 billion to health financing, bringing the total to $2.4 billion. While the dollar amount of the incentive payment was changed, the principles remained the same: additional payments to general practitioners for bulk billing were to be restricted to concession cardholders but were extended to children under sixteen years of age. New safety nets would come into operation at the level of $500 for concession cardholders and $1000 for everyone else. Finally, Medicare Plus would provide resources to increase the number of doctors by 1500 and the number of practice nurses by 1600 by the year 2006–07. In a major concession, the government abandoned the proposal to reintroduce private medical insurance. The prime minister affirmed his belief in "both the public and private elements of health care" and his government's commitment to the 30 per cent rebate. He expressed hope that the revised legislation would pass "before the Parliament rises" and called on the members of the Senate to support it.[19]

Although Medicare Plus was an improvement on a Fairer Medicare in a number of ways, it was widely criticised for two fundamentally important reasons. First, the scheme will not arrest the decline in bulk billing. Second, it is based on the assumption that Medicare will not provide universal coverage. Another major criticism levelled by John Deeble and others was that the safety net proposals will underwrite high increases in doctors' fees because the government will be committed to paying 80 per cent of whatever fees doctors choose to charge, once the threshold level is exceeded.[20] It is perhaps for this reason that the AMA gave a lukewarm welcome to the scheme, while at the same time reminding the government that its preferred policy, and one that it had campaigned on for years, is an across-the-board increase in the Medicare rebate for all medical services.

The main problems with the scheme were summarised by the health economist, Paul Gross: it affirms "the user pays principle"; the money incentive to bulk bill is unlikely to be taken up in rural and outer metropolitan areas; general practitioner charges can be expected to rise; the implications of the scheme for pensioners are unclear; low-income single persons with chronic disorders seemed to be left out; and safety net claimants will need to retain all their paperwork so they can submit their claim if and when the threshold is reached. Gross might also have mentioned the confusion that such complex arrangements cause and the very high administrative costs involved in running them. He calculated that, from user charges totalling $2000 million, Medicare Plus would return only $90 million to citizens and suggested that "some listed corporate entities will be salivating at the thought that pathology and radiology are in the safety net when bulk billing is likely to decrease."[21]

In late November, the Senate Committee on Medicare was re-established to conduct an inquiry into Medicare Plus. When it reported in February 2004 its findings were very similar, in principle, to its previous findings. Meanwhile, the bulk-billing incentive arrangements had come into operation on 1 February, implemented by ministerial determination.

For Health Minister Abbott, the first months of 2004 were absorbed with attempts to negotiate a deal with four independent senators. An agreement was finally reached in March, involving some benefits for consumers and increased outlays for the government. The Medicare Plus rebate for concession cardholders and children was fixed at a standard $5, except in Tasmania and sixteen designated rural areas, where it is $7.50. New safety nets were set at $300 for concession cardholders and $700 for everyone else; after expenses reach those levels, the government will pay 80 per cent of any fee the doctor charges above the rebate. Small, limited benefits were introduced for certain allied health services, including dentistry and physiotherapy.

Despite these additional benefits, the final version of Medicare Plus does not deal with the fundamental problems of the system: declining bulk-billing rates and rising user charges. In announcing the changes,

Minister Abbott "could not say" whether bulk-billing rates would increase or not.[22] From a cost-control perspective, the Commonwealth has made itself more vulnerable: it is committed to paying 95 per cent of whatever doctors choose to charge once a person's accumulated out-of-pocket expenses reach the safety net threshold.

In summary, during eight years of Coalition government the foundations of Medicare have been eroded. Private insurance coverage has been expanded by just under 50 per cent and covered 43.4 per cent of the population in December 2003. The prepaid public hospital system, on which Medicare-only citizens rely, remains intact but public hospital funding has been kept under tight control. Significant co-payments for out-of-hospital medical services are being paid by increasing numbers of citizens, moving funding from general revenue to private sources. Under Medicare Plus, the role of out-of-pocket financing will continue to increase, with serious implications for both access and cost control.

CHAPTER 5

Moving closer to America: increasing costs

Powerful physician organisations and large corporate actors can always inflate health care needs to meet their private income objectives as governments have slowly and painfully learned.

– DANIEL DRACHE AND TERRY SULLIVAN, 1999

In order to control anything, someone or something must be in charge. Nowhere is this commonplace more relevant than in health financing. Because forces are at work which, unchecked, give rise to exponential cost increases, cost control is an essential element of any modern health system. In tax-financed systems, governments are in charge and they have a variety of mechanisms for monitoring and, if necessary, constraining resources. In privately financed systems or in the private sectors of mixed systems, neither the government nor anyone else is in a coordinating position. Rather, a great many agencies and individual citizens pay for health care, through multiple channels, with little interaction and no planning. Individual agencies do not have the capacity to control total expenditure and, in many cases, have limited ability to control even their own outlays. Although mechanisms have been developed to try to control spending in multi-payer systems – "managed care" in the United States, for example – these have turned out to be relatively ineffective. International evidence over the last three decades demonstrates conclusively that the larger the private share of financing for hospital and medical services, the more expensive the system.[1]

All industrialised countries have at least some level of private financing. But the private sector in the United States is by far the largest in the OECD and the result is a system that costs more than any other. Does this mean that the health system in the United States is better for consumers? On the contrary, health outcomes in the US are poor when compared with other well-off nations. The country with the second-largest private health insurance sector is Switzerland, which, with health spending consuming 11.1 per cent of GDP, was the second highest spender in 2001. Private insurance covers "a sizeable proportion" of the population in Germany, the third most expensive system in 2001.[2]

In order to explain the relationship between financing systems and cost control, health economists distinguish between single-payer and multi-payer systems. Single-payer systems are predominantly publicly financed, whereas multi-payer systems are mainly privately financed through a mixture of private insurance, user charges and some level of tax funding. In single-payer systems, governments have both the power and, usually, the will to regulate budget outlays and to keep overall costs within reasonable limits. No agency has this power in multi-payer systems: the different funders are interested only in their own costs and the easiest way of reducing them is to transfer them to another payer.[3] Cost shifting replaces cost control, with expensive and regressive results.

A recent review of single-payer and multi-payer systems confirms earlier findings about their financial impact. The health economists, Peter Hussey and Gerard Anderson, found that the governments of countries with single-payer systems "essentially have total control of aggregate expenditure," usually through annual budgeting processes. Multi-payer systems, by contrast, had more difficulty monitoring and controlling expenditure because options such as global budgeting and monopsony (or exclusive) buying were not available and because "different insurers use different monitoring, payment and information systems." Costs were shifted to other payers. "Adverse selection" (where the young and healthy choose not to buy private insurance but a large proportion of those with a high risk of illness do) was found to be a serious problem in multi-payer systems but is not an issue in single-payer systems, which have a single risk pool. The mechanisms available to deal with adverse selection were found to be expensive and, according to Hussey and Anderson, "not entirely effective in practice." The study also discovered that single-payer systems were better equipped to assess technology and regulate its introduction and to control the cost of pharmaceuticals. A single-payer system also creates incentives to invest in preventive health care because beneficiaries are enrolled throughout their lives and long-term savings are possible. Finally, the study found differences in access and equity.[4]

Thus, in multi-payer systems there are typically few controls on either the volume or the price of services and procedures. Once private health insurance premiums have been paid, cost ceases to be a problem for either doctor or patient, unless insurance cover is partial, because costs are fully covered. Moreover, multi-payer systems incur much higher administrative costs than single-payer systems. As Robert Evans explains:

> Private insurers, and all who make their livings from the multitude of administrative functions that this requires, are the most obvious beneficiaries from increases in private financing. The high administrative overheads associated with private coverage are the sales revenue of this industry, and the source of its wages and profits. In [tax-funded] systems, more administratively efficient, these costs and corresponding income opportunities do not exist.[5]

A recent report showed that administrative expenses are the fastest-growing component of health expenditure in the United States, consuming $105 billion in 2002, an increase of 16.2 per cent over 2001. Administrative costs for private insurance were 12.8 per cent of total outlays compared with 3 per cent for the US Medicare scheme.[6] These differing costs are similar to those in Australia: here, private sector industry management expenses were 11.8 per cent of contribution income in 2000–01 whereas administrative expenses for Medicare were 3.6 per cent of the benefits paid.[7]

Overwhelming international evidence shows that systems with large sectors of private finance are expensive. Because the scope of private financing has been enlarged and is set to increase under Medicare Plus, the Australian health financing system is becoming more like the system in the United States. Given that this is so, it is worth taking a closer look at the operation of the American system.

•

In January 2004, Karen Davis, the president of the Commonwealth Fund, a large, private health research foundation in the US, gave evidence before the Senate Committee on Health, Education, Labor, and Pensions in Washington. She told the committee that, in 2002, national health expenditure stood at 14.9 per cent of GDP and was projected to more than double by 2012. Expenditure in 2002 was 9.3 per cent higher than in the previous year, the fastest increase in a decade. Increases in administrative costs were high. Health insurance premiums continued to rise, by 13.9 per cent in 2003, the third successive year of double-digit increases – and they would have risen by more if the funds had not narrowed coverage and increased user charges.

Private health insurance cost rises are one of the reasons for the increase in the number of uninsured people in the US. Between 2000 and 2002, their ranks grew by 9.5 per cent, from 39.8 million to 43.6 million people. The *average* premium for a family health insurance policy in 2003 was US$9068. Davis also confirmed that high health costs did not translate into more services in America; indeed, hospital visits per capita were lower than in other countries and physician visits about the same.[8] Nor, as studies over a long period have found, does high spending result in better health outcomes: a recent OECD review found health status and quality of care in the US to be "mediocre," falling considerably below what could be expected on the basis of the country's income.

Davis's list of problems did not end there. She reported that medical errors were high and the development of patient protection procedures was slow. Care was uncoordinated, research showed an enormous variation in quality and efficiency, and a recent study showed that 55 per cent of Americans did not receive the recommended care for their condition. Despite evidence of inappropriate care, no national agency existed to develop clinical guidelines.[9]

The problems of the US health system generate intense dissatisfaction, not only among consumers but also among providers.[10] Health issues became a major item in the 2004 presidential election campaign, with six candidates, including the incumbent president, proposing to extend health insurance to (some of) the uninsured.[11] A recent survey found that 49 per cent of physicians supported a national health insurance system, with only 40 per cent opposed.[12] The US Institute of Medicine has undertaken several large studies of the system and recently called for universal insurance coverage by 2010.[13] A report from the Physicians' Working Group for Single-Payer National Health Insurance, published in the *Journal of the American Medical Association*, provides a trenchant criticism of the high costs, low levels of access and poor health outcomes of the system. Echoing the findings of most other studies, the report argues that "single-source payment is the *sine qua non* of administrative simplification and the cornerstone of cost containment and health planning."[14] Karen Davis summarised the financing problems facing the US system:

> [W]e seem committed to a pluralistic system of many different private insurers and public programs, each attempting to get the best deal it can on its own, rather than a concerted effort to purchase services collectively... Other countries are more willing to use supply constraints – for example, limiting the number of physicians of different types who are permitted to practice – and to use salaried payment systems for specialists, which eliminate incentives to provide unnecessary services to generate income.[15]

She concluded that if the United States "were more willing to use the power of government to negotiate prices for medical services and prescription drugs, it could probably achieve considerably lower prices."[16]

•

Emerging Australian evidence suggests that health care costs are rising faster, as a proportion of GDP, since the Howard "reforms" than they did in the first nine years of the 1990s. But the current situation in Australia is more complex than a simple shift from public to private financing. Owing to the unusual Australian practice of direct public funding of private insurance premiums, the amount of private money finding its way into the health system has not yet increased, despite private coverage having risen by almost 50 per cent. In fact, total private funding has fallen because the taxpayer-funded 30 per cent rebate has replaced private outlays. As John Deeble argues, "the Commonwealth has simply replaced private funding with over $2 billion of its own."[17] But the fact that total private financing has not yet increased does not alter the argument about the impact of private insurance. Increased funding through private insurance encourages an expanded private hospital sector, even if 30 per cent of the cost of insurance is met from the Commonwealth purse. And, as we've seen, both governmental and health fund control is weak in the private hospital sector. If previous private hospital growth rates persist – and there is every reason to expect they will – the open-ended reimbursement system will fuel cost increases.

The latest figures from the Australian Institute of Health and Welfare show that health spending increased faster after 1998–99 than it had in the previous eight years. Expenditure increased at roughly the same rate as GDP between 1991–92 and 1998–99. After that year, however, a gap began to open up, with health expenditure growing faster than GDP. Expenditure was 9.1 per cent of GDP in 2000–01, rising to 9.3 per cent in 2001–02 and estimates indicate that the gap will continue to increase. Institute figures show that real health expenditures grew by an average of 5.7 per cent each year after 1998–99, compared with real GDP growth of 3.2 per cent.[18]

Australia is spending more on health than ever before, both in absolute terms and as a proportion of GDP. In the 1980s and 1990s, Australian spending was almost exactly in line with the OECD average. In 2001, however, Australia moved ahead: the OECD average remained steady at 8.4 per cent of GDP while Australian expenditures had risen to 9.2 per cent. Recent increases, the institute found, are due to "a combination of volume and price effects," an outcome consistent with the impact of increased private financing.[19] The institute anticipates a continuing increase in the ratio of health expenditure to GDP.

Evidence from the operation of Medicare shows that health costs are rising more rapidly in the private sector than in the public. In a major study of costs in the first seven years of Medicare, John Deeble found that expenditure had been successfully restrained in the sectors the government controlled, with costs rising faster in the areas outside public control. Between 1984 and 1991, costs increased by 49 per cent in hospitals, nursing homes, community health and research. In contrast, costs rose by 64 per cent in the private hospital, medical services and dentistry areas.[20]

The price of medical services – the services delivered by doctors – has risen more sharply in the private sector than in the public. In a study of Medicare outlays for medical services, John Deeble found that in 1994–95 insured in-hospital medical services were billed at an average of 17.1 per cent above the Medicare schedule fee, compared with average fees of only 99.8 per cent of the schedule for out-of-hospital services. According to Deeble, this shows that doctors' charging practices for in-hospital, privately insured patients were influenced by the availability of gap insurance for 100 per cent coverage of the schedule fee.[21] In other words, this mechanism did not benefit patients in the longer term, because specialists, mainly surgeons and procedural specialists, increased their fees to take advantage of the high level of cover offered by private insurance. The introduction of gap insurance to cover fees higher than the schedule for privately insured, in-hospital medical services can only exacerbate this situation.

By 2000–01, average in-hospital overbilling had doubled to 34 per cent above the schedule fee. Although full gap insurance is now allowed under certain circumstances, less than 40 per cent of total overbilling is covered because the doctors who overcharge the most are the slowest to enter into fee agreements with health funds. Average billing under "no-gap" or "known-gap" arrangements was approximately 23 per cent above the schedule fee in 2002.[22]

Ultimately, higher medical fees in the private sector must also affect the price that Medicare pays for medical services in public hospitals, inflating public sector costs as well. As health economists Stephen Duckett and Terri Jackson point out, higher fees in the private sector "create problems for recruitment of medical specialists in the public sector and probably inflate public sector medical remuneration."[23]

Evidence suggests that private hospital treatment is more expensive than public. Duckett and Jackson's study found that the private health insurance rebate was an inefficient way of assisting public hospitals for this reason. After adjusting for patient case-mix and differences in financing elements, they found that public hospitals are able to treat patients at 91 per cent of the cost of private hospital care. They concluded that "there does not appear to be a strong argument for public sector subsidy to the private sector based on its greater technical efficiency." Treatment in the private sector, they added, "is associated with higher rates of intervention, with no demonstrable impact on outcome or quality."[24] A recent study by James Pearse and his colleagues corroborates this finding: they found that between

1997–98 and 2002–03, private health insurance benefits per bed day increased by 29.9 per cent for private hospitals, compared with a 17 per cent increase for public hospitals.[25]

The Pearse study found "significant inflation" in prices paid for hospital services, medical services and prostheses in the private hospital sector. In the period from 1997–98 to 2002–03, overall benefits paid by the private health insurance funds increased by approximately 70 per cent, partly because of increased membership after Lifetime Health Cover came into operation. However, when adjusted for the age composition of the new membership and the utilisation rates at the time, it was found that the effect of higher prices had pushed up expenditures by 50 per cent.[26]

Utilisation rates in the private hospital sector are higher than in the public sector and appear to be increasing. In 1997–98, admission rates for privately insured people were 274 per thousand persons, compared with 254 for the Medicare population.[27] When the different cost rates and utilisation rates are combined, John Deeble calculates a higher private sector cost of around 14 per cent. Therefore, the 50 per cent increase in private insurance coverage that has taken place since the beginning of 1999 can be expected to raise total hospital expenditures by about 2.1 per cent.[28] This is not a spectacular increase but nor is it to be disregarded.

•

Assessments by leading health economists of the 30 per cent taxpayer subsidy for private insurance show that it has failed in its main aim: to take pressure off the public hospital system. One analysis suggests that it may even have increased the pressure. The Howard government and the major medical bodies argued that the decline in private health insurance coverage between 1984 and 1998 had led to a lower use of private hospitals, which increased pressure on the public hospital system, creating queues and increasing waiting lists. Expanding the private sector, they argued, would relieve the pressure and make more room for Medicare patients. The health economist Jeff Richardson has shown that this analysis is "for the most part wrong."[29] In the nine years between 1989–90 and 1998–99, private health insurance revenue rose by 54.8 per cent and private hospital income by 135 per cent – nearly double the increase in public hospital spending. Private hospitals increased their share of "separations" (hospital admissions) by 32 per cent. Thus, private insurance coverage may have declined but private hospital income and private hospital activity increased significantly. In Richardson's view, public hospital waiting lists increased over the period for three reasons: there was a shortage of certain specialists; hospitals were favouring private over public patients; and state governments had been successful in limiting public hospital expenditures.

Of course, it could be argued that public hospital waiting times would have been longer without these increases in private hospital activity. And this may be so. But it is important to remember that Australians are among the highest users of hospital services in the world, 55 per cent higher than Canadians and 30 per cent higher than citizens of the United States.[30] Exactly what drives Australia's high hospitalisation rates is unclear. But it is surely open to question whether those rates need to be increased any further. Private hospital services are a lucrative source of income for providers.

Moreover, John Deeble has shown that only 40 per cent of the increased benefits paid out by private insurers after 1998–99 was directed towards health services which would help reduce pressure on the public health system. The other 60 per cent went towards higher ancillary benefits, including gym shoes and the like, upgraded private hospital insurance coverage and the extension of gap insurance coverage.[31]

Jeff Richardson argues that although the government's private health insurance policies have not been fully analysed, the impact may have been perverse, in the sense of increasing pressure on the public hospital system. The reason is simple: the number of doctors and nurses moving to the private sector may be greater than any transfer of patients. Anecdotal evidence suggests, for example, that surgery is being postponed in public hospitals because of a shortage of anaesthetists, even when surgeons are available. Anaesthetists are heavily occupied in private sector work and their bulk-billing rate is extremely low, at approximately 5 per cent. Richardson cites evidence to show that patients treated in private hospitals after heart attacks are between two and four times as likely to receive intensive treatment as public hospital patients. If this is so, he argues, then a 10 per cent transfer of patients would be accompanied by a 20 per cent transfer of medical personnel, increasing rather than reducing pressures in the public sector. Such a proposition is highly plausible, Richardson suggests, because there is "a strong financial incentive to give a larger number of more complex services in the profitable fee-for-service, private sector than in the less profitable, salaried or sessional, public sector."[32]

A study by the economist, Ian McAuley, in 2004 reached similar conclusions. To the extent that the rebate has paid for hospital services, it has gone primarily to those who were using private hospitals anyway. It is an expensive way to support private hospitals and has not relieved pressure on public hospitals, which still have to provide care for the complex cases which the private sector cannot handle. Resources, especially skilled staff, have been drawn away from the public sector and McAuley concludes that the inflationary impact of private insurance places a heavy cost burden on the system as a whole.[33]

Richardson's and McAuley's propositions are supported by a recent study of the Australian situation by a team of economists led by Jeremiah Hurley, who found that queuing times in the public hospital sector had not shortened since 1999. They point out that the public and private sectors do not operate in isolation from each other – instead, "numerous tendrils inevitably entwine them" – and they report international evidence which suggests that the existence of parallel health sectors "actually increase[s] wait times, especially when providers can work simultaneously in both the public and private sectors."[34]

Strong, parallel private sectors have been found to have other adverse consequences for public sectors. Well-funded private facilities can set an unrealistically opulent standard for their public counterparts, forcing public providers to "reconfigure both their organisational structure and their activities in the image of private sector facilities," according to the economists Richard Saltman and Casten Van Otter.[35] Public sectors come under pressure to alter their mix of services and to abolish preventive, educational, counselling and referral services and primary care strategies. In order to keep pace with the services marketed in the image-conscious private sector, the capacity to pursue difficult long-term objectives may be lost. Saltman and

Van Otter conclude that "public providers come to mirror their privately capitalised, profit oriented counterparts."

In the United States, another adverse effect of this cost spiral is an increase in the number of people who are uninsured. In Australia, as insurance costs rise people drop private cover and turn back to the public system. This dynamic was amply demonstrated when the Fraser government tried to manage a mixed public and private financing system in the 1970s. Under Medibank Mark 2, as the scheme was called, consumers were entitled to opt out of public health insurance (and escape the obligation to pay the health insurance levy) if they purchased private insurance. Incentives were put in place with the intention of achieving a 50–50 balance between the public and private sectors and, initially, this balance was achieved.[36] But as private sector costs rose, the price of insurance escalated and people increasingly chose to move back to Medibank. Major private sector interest groups pressed the government to take action and the AMA claimed that the health system was "slowly bleeding to death."[37] The system was so unstable that the last public elements of Medibank were eventually abolished altogether.

The early stages of a similar process have unfolded since 2001. The private health insurance industry as a whole lost $60 million in 2001–02.[38] In early 2002, several large funds applied to the Department of Health and Ageing for permission to increase premiums. Despite the government's effort to keep increases to 3 per cent or less – the general rate of inflation at the time – private health insurance premiums increased by an average of 6.9 per cent in 2002. Premiums again increased in 2003, this time by an average of 7.4 per cent across the industry.[39] A number of funds also substantially increased the user charges payable by contributors, without which the price of insurance premiums would have increased by more.

According to Russell Schneider, chief executive of the Australian Health Insurance Association, people who are privately insured must be prepared to put up with health care inflation if they want access to "modern health care."[40] The Private Health Insurance Administration Council reported that total benefits paid out by the funds increased by 15.8 per cent in 2001–02, with an increase in benefits for prostheses of 41 per cent and in gap-cover payments of 18.3 per cent.[41] Premium increases for 2004 averaged 7.58 per cent, a further increase over 2003 and way ahead of the general inflation rate. Gap payments to doctors increased by 33.3 per cent in 2002–03, by far the largest increase of any component, followed by an increase of 28 per cent for prostheses. In other words, providers are doing rather well. Rising premiums are coinciding with a slow but steady decline in the number of people holding private insurance.

A recent OECD review of private health insurance confirms the international experience. The review found that the new Australian regime makes controlling costs more difficult and creates regulatory tensions. Subsidies to private health cover, the study observed, place "considerable pressures on public finances." Corroborating previous research, it found that private health insurance appears to have promoted an increase in overall hospital usage and that, while mechanisms are in place to control cost increases in the public sector, such mechanisms are "not well-developed" in the private hospital sector. The report points out that private insurance funds do not try to control hospital use or to limit claims growth. The study found that gap insurance had an inflationary effect, in some cases of up to 50 per cent. It identified higher private sector administrative costs and noted that medical devices had become an area of cost growth after the government deregulated prices. The report noted that private hospitals still offer a more limited range of services than public hospitals and that, consequently, "the costs of high-risk patients" and "high-cost emergency and complex procedures are left with the public system."[42]

Echoing the studies mentioned earlier in this chapter, the OECD report found a strong growth in the cost of private health insurance, attributing this to a combination of the impact of gap cover, the higher cost of prostheses and increased utilisation. It argued that, despite the 30 per cent rebate, affordability will decline if the cost of premiums keeps rising and noted that "as long as cost inflation in this sector is unrestrained, premiums are likely to continue to rise."[43] In conclusion, the report says:

> Private funds have not effectively engaged in cost controls. They seem to have limited tools and few incentives to promote cost-efficient care, and there are margins for some funds to improve administrative

> efficiency, thereby reducing administrative costs. PHI [private health insurance] appears to have led to an overall increase in health utilisation in Australia as there are limited constraints on expenditure growth. Insurers are not exposed to the risk of managing the entire continuum of care... Policies to reduce medical gaps have led to some price increase and may have enhanced supply-side moral hazard incentives. Finally, the rebate on PHI premiums has posed pressures on public cost, as it represents tax resources that have alternative uses.[44]

International evidence clearly shows that the most effective way of restraining cost increases is through a single-payer, tax-funded system. Before 1996, the role of private finance was steadily declining but that process has been reversed by the policies introduced over the past eight years. Australia now displays many more of the features of a multi-payer model, with a large sector of private financing which has few cost controls.

CHAPTER 6

Moving closer to America: decreasing access

The more heavily a national system relies on private financing, the larger the proportion of overall health care costs that will be borne by those with lower incomes.

– Robert G. Evans, 2002

Just as there is a large body of international evidence of the impact of private financing on health care costs, so there is a large body of evidence about the impact of user charges on the use of health services. User charges are a major source of private financing, of course, and study after study shows clearly that they deter people from using health services. By failing to prevent the long-term decline of bulk billing and by insisting that incentives are to be restricted to concession cardholders, the Howard government has presided over the growth of user charges as a method of paying for care and ensured that this component of financing will expand over time. In so doing, it is moving Australia closer to the United States, where user charges are excessively high.

A shift from public to private financing doesn't only increase barriers to access, however. It also changes the burden of responsibility for health care costs, benefiting some groups but disadvantaging others. Public financing is "progressive" because taxation is generally levied according to income. Private financing does not share this feature: health insurance premiums, full-cost payments and user fees are charged at a flat rate and take no account of people's ability to pay. In a health system that is primarily financed from taxation, those in the higher income groups contribute more while those further down the income ladder contribute less. When health is increasingly funded from private sources, this progressive effect is reversed.

The growing role of private health insurance as a financing mechanism is even more regressive in its Australian manifestation. First, although private insurance reduces the need for taxation revenue, one third of the cost of premiums is met from taxation through the rebate. People on low incomes generally do not buy private insurance and are therefore excluded from the benefits of the subsidy. As costs in the private sector increase, taxpayers in general get to pay for a third of the cost of the care consumed by the (mostly high-income) privately insured.

But there is even worse news. Because there is a strong connection between low income and ill health, an increase in private sources of funding decreases the proportion of health care costs paid by the healthy and increases the proportion paid by the sick. As the Canadian economist, Bob Evans, has pointed out, "if one holds total health outlays – and everything else – constant, and shifts the mix of revenue sources by raising user fees and lowering taxes, the effect is to transfer income from the unhealthy and unwealthy to the healthy and wealthy."[1] In other words, the Howard government's policies have eroded the fundamental principle of Medicare: that we should contribute to health care costs according to our ability to pay.

•

Over the past couple of decades, a series of international and Australian studies has looked at the impact of user charges on the level and pattern of consumers' use of health care services. Not surprisingly, the studies have demonstrated that when health consumers are charged for access they use fewer services, especially if they are living on low incomes. Significantly, the studies also show that consumers do not simply cut down on ineffective or discretionary health care – they are forced by user charges to reduce consultations and procedures across the board.

These two messages recur through the literature on access to care. According to a survey of the results of the famous RAND health insurance experiment, one of the largest social science surveys ever conducted, user charges reduced both "appropriate and inappropriate services – or highly efficacious and relatively inefficacious services – by the same proportion."[2]

In 1991 Jeff Richardson reviewed the international evidence for the Australian National Health Strategy. He concluded that user charges had a significant impact on "demand" for services and, in the absence of other influences, co-payments of 25 to 30 per cent reduced utilisation by about the same percentage.[3] Three years later, in a report undertaken for the Ontario Premier's Council on Health, Greg Stoddart, Morris Barer and Robert Evans found that "charges did not lead to reduction in utilisation of only unnecessary or less necessary services but affect the utilisation of needed services as well." For some groups, they found, both the financial and health effects were potentially serious.[4]

User charges have a greater impact on low-income people and an adverse effect on health outcomes. Although the RAND study did not find a strong association between usage and income (it excluded the elderly, a higher proportion of whom are poor, and the charges paid by the poor were reduced) later studies show this linkage. Even small charges, it seems, represent a significant proportion of income for those who are not well-off. Three studies of Medicaid beneficiaries in the United States surveyed by Thomas Rice and Kathleen Morrison found that small user charges reduced visits to general practitioners and resulted in higher rates of hospitalisation.[5]

The point is even more vividly illustrated in cases where charges have been removed or imposed in a single policy shift. When the National Health Service was introduced in Britain and Medicare introduced in Quebec, the abolition of user charges resulted in a shift of services away from high-income groups towards those on low incomes. But when user charges were reintroduced in the province of Saskatchewan in the 1970s, the use of services fell by between 6 and 7 per cent across the board and by 12 per cent for those defined as poor. For the very poor – families who spent 70 per cent or more of their incomes on food, clothing and shelter – the decline in usage was 18 per cent.[6]

A more recent set of studies during the late 1990s, particularly in the United States, confirmed the earlier findings. Work in New

Zealand found that 14 per cent of women and 12 per cent of men felt they had needed to see a doctor in the previous year but had not. About half of them identified cost as the reason. People in lower income groups were found to be less likely to visit dentists, dental nurses, opticians and physiotherapists. One in ten adults had not collected a prescription item in the previous year, and cost emerged as the main reason. A second New Zealand study showed significant levels of avoidable mortality and morbidity and concluded that, of the almost one third of hospitalisations in the 0–74 age group that could have been avoided, two thirds could have been avoided through more effective primary care services.[7]

The Commonwealth Fund, in conjunction with researchers at the Harvard School of Public Health, has conducted a number of five-nation comparative studies of various aspects of health experience in Australia, Canada, New Zealand, the United Kingdom and the United States. Sharp disparities were found in access to health care in the United States. People on below-average incomes are three times more likely to report having difficulty accessing medical care than those on higher incomes. Disparities were also found in Australia and New Zealand, however, and again low-income groups faced the greatest difficulties. Fourteen per cent of Australians on below-average incomes and 24 per cent of New Zealanders on below-average incomes reported problems in paying for medical bills. Difficulties were far less marked for above-average income groups but were not negligible.[8] Another survey found that financial barriers to access were highest in the United States but also existed in all the other countries. Again, problems were more common among low-income groups.[9]

A proliferation of recent studies in the United States, only a few of which can be reviewed here, reveal that access is poor and deteriorating quickly. Moreover, health outcomes are seriously affected. One study found an "unhappy confluence of accelerated premiums, sharply increased cost sharing, and declining coverage."[10] In 2002, 80 per cent of the uninsured were from families in which the head of the household was in full-time or part-time work. Uninsured people are less likely to go to the doctor in the first place, more likely to have long waits for specialist services, less likely to receive medications and treatments, and less likely to use preventive services. Not surprisingly, disparities in care are greater among people with chronic health problems.[11] Further, as one study records, "despite a wide range of safety net health programs, uninsured persons are less likely to receive care when they really need it and, as a result, experience significant morbidity and excess mortality."[12] Meanwhile, the US Institute of Medicine has produced a number of recent reports showing that people without insurance, including pregnant women, newborn infants and children, avoid seeking care, use fewer services and have poorer health.[13] The institute has estimated that 18,000 adults between the ages of 25 and 64 die each year "as a direct result of being uninsured."[14] A 2003 report estimated that the cost of premature death and illness from lack of health insurance was perhaps as high as $130 billion a year.[15]

All of this evidence shows a strong association between user charges, a lack of access to health services and adverse health outcomes. Of course, a lack of access to medical care is not the only, or even the most important, determinant of ill health, as we will see in the next chapter, and barriers to access in Australia are not yet as severe as those in the United States. But there is nevertheless cause for serious concern. Statistics show that per capita user charges in Australia were the third highest in the OECD in 2001, lower only than those of Switzerland and the United States, the two countries with the highest levels of private financing.[16] The situation can only become worse as bulk-billing rates decline further under present policies.

In 2003, the Royal Australian College of General Practitioners reported "consistent anecdotal feedback" from members suggesting that the people most in need of care are at risk of being denied access because of user charges. In its submission to the Senate, the college used the recent five-nation studies, mentioned above, to argue that costs are "a leading reason why Australians do not follow their doctor's advice" and that many people do not visit their general practitioners, except for "sickness care."[17] In another study, Robert Blendon and his colleagues found that, owing to cost, 21 per cent of Australians with below-average incomes did not fill prescriptions, 17 per cent did not get a recommended test, treatment or follow-up consultation, 14 per cent reported that they had a medical problem but did not visit the doctor, and 17 per cent reported problems paying medical bills.[18] A later study found that 41 per cent of Australians had difficulty seeing a specialist, with 17 per cent naming cost as the reason. Twenty-three per cent of people had not filled a prescription and 44 per cent had not accessed dental care for the same reason.[19]

The shift to private insurance is changing the makeup of the Australian hospital system and reducing access to elective surgery for Medicare patients. A 2003 report for the Royal Australasian College of Surgeons presented evidence of a shift of elective surgery from public to private hospitals. It noted that public hospitals tend to focus on treating life-threatening conditions, with waiting lists for non-urgent surgery. According to the college, people without private insurance can no longer expect to get elective surgery in the public hospital system and even the privately insured from rural and regional Australia have to go to metropolitan hospitals for surgery. The report suggested that there is an "increase in demand for surgical services" and estimated a rise in demand of 50 per cent by 2021. The college predicts that as people realise they cannot get access to elective surgery in public hospitals, there will be "increased pressure" on them to take out private insurance, thereby boosting "demand." In "a couple of years," it says, there will be no guarantee that any doctors will work in the public system "as there will be absolutely no financial incentive to do so."[20] To the extent that this snapshot of emerging trends is accurate, it gives cause for concern: citizens reliant on Medicare will have increasingly limited access to elective surgery and, as in the past, many will undergo hardship to pay outright or to pay for private insurance.

New evidence from the NSW Department of Health researcher, Paul Tridgell, supports the college's findings. Private patients, the data show, are using the lion's share of non-emergency surgery: they are twice as likely, on average, to have access to elective hospital treatment. Private patients are undergoing six times as many gynaecological surgical procedures, twice the number of cataract operations and gastroscopies and 2.6 times the number of colonoscopies. Approximately half of the cost of these procedures is borne by general taxpayers through a combination of Medicare payments, private insurance and pharmaceutical subsidies. Increased elective surgery in private hospitals has been accompanied by a small rise in emergency procedures in public hospitals and a fall in emergency procedures in the private sector.[21]

The growth in user charges is also uneven, affecting different groups of health consumers in different ways. The eighteen electorates with the highest bulk-billing rates in 2003 were in metropolitan areas. Conversely, eighteen of the twenty electorates with the lowest bulk-billing rates in 2003 were in provincial or rural areas. Between 2000 and 2003, bulk-billing rates declined by 10 per cent or more in only 14 of the 40 richest (and overwhelmingly inner-metropolitan) electorates. Twenty-three of these electorates had bulk-billing rates of 70 per cent or more and six had some of the highest levels in the country, with rates of over 90 per cent. In contrast, of the 40 poorest electorates, overwhelmingly rural and provincial, all but twelve either already had very low rates of bulk billing in 2000 or experienced a decline of 20 per cent or more between 2000 and 2003. In four of the twelve remaining electorates, bulk-billing rates fell by 15 per cent or more.[22]

Thus, an ironic picture emerges. Bulk-billing rates are relatively stable and relatively high in most of the well-off inner-metropolitan areas (where doctors prefer to practise) but very low or falling quickly in the poorest electorates (where doctors prefer not to practise). People who are healthier and wealthier are quite likely to be able to find a bulk-billing general practitioner; people who are poorer and have a higher incidence of ill health will probably be asked to pay user fees. The regressive impact of the move away from tax funding and towards user charges is exacerbated by the location of doctors willing to bulk bill.

These findings coincide with evidence presented to the second Senate inquiry into Medicare. Medical experts told the committee that life expectancy for people living in the country is lower than in the city, and that "if you are poor and/or live outside a major city, you are more likely to get seriously ill and to die younger than the rest of the population." Research for 1998 shows that if everyone had the same level of health as the highest 20 per cent of income earners, about 180,000 life years would be saved every year and there would have been about 800,000 fewer disabled people in 1998. This would save about $4 billion a year in taxpayer outlays on health costs and disability support schemes. Moreover, the committee argued that "if you live in the poorer suburbs of Sydney's outer-west region you are five times more likely to die prematurely from what doctors can demonstrate to be largely preventable problems than if you live on Sydney's more affluent north-shore."[23]

A final concern, expressed by groups such as the Doctors Reform Society and picked up in the 2003 OECD study of Australia, is that concession cardholders may be stigmatised because they are "non-paying" patients. Receptionists might have to ask intrusive questions, with the risk that doctors' offices might turn into branches of the means-tested welfare system. Catholic Health Australia argues that families on meagre incomes will be the real losers: in any means-tested system, those who narrowly fail to qualify for concession status are required to pay full fees.[24] As the health economist Stephen Duckett has argued:

> Means testing will always cause problems at the margin – as families drift in and out of employment, their entitlements for the new stigmatised services will wax and wane, leaving them in a state of uncertainty about seeking treatment, with the risk of cost blowouts because of the failure to obtain early care.[25]

A simple message emerges from all these studies. As user charges grow, both in number and size, cost barriers are being placed between Australian citizens and medical services. Nothing in either A Fairer Medicare or Medicare Plus was intended to reverse this trend, except (perhaps) for concession cardholders and children. Moreover, there is evidence that as the private hospital sector grows, stimulated by the rebate, fewer physicians will be willing to work in the public hospital system. Under the Howard government's policies, user charges have been entrenched as one of the principal financing mechanisms, replacing tax funding, a move which is recognised internationally as highly regressive. The vice-president of the Doctors Reform Society, Tracy Schrader, has summarised the case against co-payments:

> A health care payment system relying heavily on co-payments… will result in a less equitable system with more health costs met from average household incomes instead of taxation. It can readily be demonstrated that co-payments financially advantage both the wealthy and doctors. Under the government's proposal… the most

> affluent in society will have better access yet pay less overall; and users – usually the sick, young families and those on a low income – will have worse access and higher costs. Any transfer of payment for health-care from taxation to user fees benefits the wealthy... Cost sharing schemes are complex, expensive to administer and likely to increase the total cost of the health-care system.[26]

•

Australians have reacted strongly to the decline in bulk billing and increases in user charges. New groups have formed and many established groups have rallied around Medicare. Indeed, the only groups that seem to favour the changes are the Coalition parties and the private health insurance industry. Among doctors' groups, all the major associations – the Australian Medical Association, the Royal Australian College of General Practitioners, the Royal Australasian College of Surgeons, the Royal Australasian College of Physicians, the Doctors Reform Society and the Rural Doctors Association of Australia – opposed A Fairer Medicare. The bigger groups have, however, accepted Medicare Plus because it will result in higher medical incomes with no restraints on fees. Most medical groups argue that there is a crisis in general practice which the proposals fail to solve. Reimbursement levels are so low that practices will continue to struggle, they say, and the schedule fee should be doubled.[27]

Specialists, annoyed by the focus on general practice, argue that their needs have been ignored. They point out that specialists who bulk bill are very poorly reimbursed compared with those who do not. In fact, very few specialists other than physicians bulk bill. The latest Senate inquiry found that in the September quarter of 2003, only 27 per cent of specialist visits were bulk billed. In obstetrics, the level was 19.3 per cent, in anaesthetics 9.3 per cent and in diagnostic imaging 58.8 per cent. The greatest decline since 1984 has been in the number of specialists who charge at the level of the schedule fee. In 1984–85, only 21 per cent of specialist services were bulk billed but another 52 per cent were charged at the level of the schedule fee. This means that, at that time, over half of all specialist services incurred a user charge of only 15 per cent. In 2002–03, the proportion of bulk-billed specialist services was a little higher at 27 per cent but the proportion charged at the level of the schedule fee had fallen dramatically to 14 per cent. Charges levied at a modest rate are now a small proportion of the total. Some 51 per cent of specialist services incur high or very high user charges.[28] The Senate committee recommended that the government encourage more specialists to bulk bill or charge the schedule fee by negotiating agreements on fees. Where such agreements are "impractical," the committee suggested the government explore other options for the provision of services.[29] Minister Abbott, however, has ruled out such action because "we don't believe in medical conscription and we don't believe in a whole new raft of price controls on doctors."[30]

Two groups of doctors have criticised the government's scheme from a pro-Medicare perspective. The Doctors Reform Society, which has actively campaigned against all of the Howard government's health policy changes, has been joined by the Royal Australasian College of Physicians, which is arguing strongly in favour of retaining universality. (Bulk billing is relatively popular among physicians, who, on average, charge just below the schedule fee.) According to the college:

> International evidence supports universal health care... Medicare must not become only a safety net for the "poor" with the more "well off" being "encouraged" to use the private system... [A]t the present rate of decline, bulk billing will disappear within a few years. Some urgent and cost-effective reforms are necessary to save Medicare and bulk billing.[31]

Activist community groups include the National Medicare Alliance, which was formed in 1998. Its members are the Australian Council of Social Service, the Public Health Association of Australia, the Australian Consumers' Association, the Australian Women's Health Network, the Australian Nursing Federation, the Health Issues Centre and the Doctors Reform Society. Similar composite groups have formed at the state and territory level in New South Wales, Victoria and the Australian Capital Territory. A new National Rural Health Alliance brings together 24 groups, including doctors and nurses and groups representing Aboriginal people, women and religious organisations. The Australian Council of Trade Unions has developed a campaign and state-based union groups have also mobilised.

A second major national grouping, the Australian Health Reform Alliance, formed in 2003. It represents 22 health and consumer organisations. The main aim of this group was to influence the Australian Health Care Agreements, through which Commonwealth health funding is transferred to the states and territories. Agreements covering the next five years were signed in 2003. The alliance called for a major increase in Commonwealth funding for public hospitals, which it claims are in crisis, and for the establishment of a Health Care Commission, which would preside over future policy changes. Along with most other community-based groups, the alliance supports the redirection of the 30 per cent private health insurance rebate to Medicare.[32]

A detailed plan for reallocating the cost of the rebate – upwards of $2.3 billion – has been drawn up by the Doctors Reform Society. The society argues that $280 million should be used to increase the schedule fee for general practitioner consultations, $80 million allocated to practice support payments for those doctors who bulk bill everyone and $100 million used to establish multidisciplinary, primary health care centres staffed by salaried doctors. Public hospitals would get $710 million, representing a funding increase of 10 per cent, $300 million would be allocated to aged care and $120 million to Aboriginal health (an increase of 10 per cent), and $750 million would be spent on re-establishing the Commonwealth dental health scheme. The remaining $160 million would be allocated to a program to educate doctors about optimal prescribing practices to reduce pressure from the pharmaceutical industry on the pharmaceutical benefits scheme.[33]

As well as the range of community groups that have gathered around Medicare, the Democrats and the Greens opposed the Howard government's 2003 proposals, although the Democrats did not oppose all of the earlier privatisation measures. The Democrats argued that A Fairer Medicare would take health care back to the 1960s and that the package would inevitably lead to price increases across the whole health system. In time, they say, price increases force more people to take out private insurance, even if it causes hardship.[34]

Widespread community concern was also reflected in the number of submissions made to the first Senate inquiry into Medicare. Despite a short deadline, the committee received 190 written submissions from diverse individuals and groups and the reconstituted committee received another batch. Community concern was also reflected in opinion polls during 2003, which suggested that there was little support for the changes before parliament. An ACNielsen poll, taken soon after A Fairer Medicare was announced, showed that only 14 per cent of people believed the package would improve the health system, with 41 per cent expressing the belief that the changes would lead to a worse system and 45 per cent unsure whether the changes would make any difference. The high "don't know" rate seemed to be a reflection of the complexity of the issues and the contradictory arguments that had been widely publicised. Even among Coalition supporters, only 16 per cent approved of the changes, 28 per cent thought the system would be made worse and the remainder, 56 per cent, didn't know if the changes would make a difference.[35] Another poll, taken by the same company in the same month, found that only 29 per cent of people thought the government's Medicare policies were better than those of the Labor Party, while 38 per cent of people favoured Labor's proposals. This poll showed strong general support for government spending on community services: 77 per cent of people said they would prefer the 2003 tax cuts ($10.7 billion over four years) to be spent on health and education.[36] In response to a survey conducted by the Democrats, which asked whether the rebate money should be redirected to strengthen Medicare, 78 per cent of people said "yes," 16.5 per cent said "no" and 5.5 per cent were unsure.[37]

•

In this debate the role and attitudes of the main medical unions are complex. Like the political parties, the Royal Australian College of General Practitioners does not have a clear position on the public–private financing mix. Because it has not addressed the tensions between the financial autonomy of medical practitioners and the principle of universal access, its arguments are not entirely consistent. It is critical of the barriers to access created by co-payments but argues for a continuation of fee-for-service private medical practice. It strongly supports "the provision of a safety net for those who find themselves unable to afford primary medical care" without acknowledging that safety nets are redundant in universal systems. It takes the position that "it is the government's responsibility to ensure universal access to primary medical care," presumably through the uncapped reimbursement of fees chosen by practitioners, a highly expensive option.[38]

The AMA, likewise, argues that access is being jeopardised by current policy and is concerned that "those who can afford to pay [will] get treated ahead of patients who need to be bulk billed." The association also strongly supports fee-for-service private practice and doctors' rights to set their own fees. In probably the most artful claim of 2003, the AMA argued that "there is now ample evidence that the health of people in areas with doctor shortages is worse than in those areas with an adequate level of medical services," as though it has not always been the case that (most) doctors prefer not to locate in areas inhabited by the sick and the poor, regardless of financial incentives.[39] The claim also suggests a direct connection between low levels of medical services and poor health status, which we know to be only partly true. According to the College of General Practitioners, the reasons that medical graduates are reluctant to work in disadvantaged areas include "professional isolation, partners' careers, children's education needs, high on-call burdens and difficulty gaining access to local hospitals."[40]

The AMA and the Australian Divisions of General Practice (ADGP) both called for large increases in the schedule fee for general practitioner services in the 2003 budget. The ADGP appears to have been active in trying to accelerate the decline of bulk billing. The Senate Estimates Committee was told that in February 2003 the organisation had staged a meeting in Melbourne, sponsored by the Pfizer drug company, to educate doctors on how to "move away from bulk billing." The chair of the ADGP, Dr Rob Walters, told the Senate committee that he would defend "the right of doctors to discuss whatever they want."[41]

CHAPTER 7

Health: the issue that rarely rates a mention

Achieving and maintaining health are not just matters of curing illness... On the eve of the 21st-century, a power struggle emerges between the god of medical art, Panakeia, who is growing increasingly ambitious and skilful in her attempts to resurrect the dead, and Hygeia, the goddess of public health and great priestess of social reforms.

– MARC RENAUD, 1994

What seems like health policy debate in Australia is, in reality, a debate about how to finance a set of services – and these services are not really health services at all. They are primarily a set of hospital and medical services used by people almost exclusively after they become ill. They are important services, of course, but they are not the only services that a health system should provide.

At present, the vast bulk of "health" spending in OECD countries is devoted to hospital and medical services. Very little is spent on public health or on prevention and promotion activities. In the United States, 95 per cent of the trillion dollars spent on health goes directly to medical care services; in Australia, 74 per cent of total health expenditure in 2000–01 was spent on hospitals, medical fees, medicines and high-level residential aged care.[1] According to the Australian Institute of Health and Welfare, less than 2 per cent of all health expenditure is directed to public health. But, as the head of the institute's Health and Welfare Expenditure Unit, Tony Hynes, has pointed out, "spending money on public health is a type of investment that puts a brake on future spending. There is a double pay off – people enjoy better health... and this spending actually leads to reduced need in the future for the more costly treatment services."[2]

It has been known for many years that curative medical services are not the most important determinant of good health.[3] In the 1970s, Thomas McKeown showed that the significant increases in life expectancy in Britain in the previous century had resulted not from biomedical interventions but from better nutrition, housing and hygiene.[4] In the United States in 1995, John Bunker and his colleagues estimated that curative medicine has accounted for only three of the seven years by which life expectancy has increased since 1950.[5] Moreover, unequivocal evidence has existed for decades showing that modern health systems have not reduced inequalities in health status.[6] Health (rather than health financing) experts have argued consistently that population health could be improved if a wider range of integrated, preventive, caring and support services were available and the social environment improved. Reforms like these, however, would disturb existing power distributions. Health care delivery systems would need to be reorganised and funds reallocated – changes that would be strongly resisted by the interest groups embedded in the hospital and medical care industries.

In this respect, Australia is not significantly different from comparable countries. All modern systems are to some extent hospital-centred and the main focus of health reform in most OECD countries has been cost control, rather than health. There is a serious dilemma here for governments and the citizens they represent, the response to which will shape health systems in the years to come. The dilemma is whether to act on the evidence and implement population health strategies or whether to continue to underwrite the expansion of systems based on the biological and medical sciences. Both directions involve governments in heavy political risks.

Health already consumes, on average, almost one dollar in every ten in OECD countries, and has the propensity to continue to expand, seemingly without end. Almost twenty years ago, it was calculated that 50,000 Americans a year would benefit from an artificial heart but that providing that one operation alone would cost at least $3 billion in

1985 prices.[7] Nearly three decades later, the choice of new procedures is much wider. The sociologist Marc Renaud has painted a striking picture of merging biological and technological developments, including regular grafts of tired organs, pills to restore libidinal balance and deal with wrinkles and senescence, procedures allowing parents to choose the characteristics of newborns, and a proliferation of personal medical monitoring devices.[8] Gene therapy is expected to become a major part of medicine in the 21st century, drawing in congenital, hereditary, psychiatric and behavioural conditions once considered outside the scope of medical science.[9] A multinational biotechnology industry has emerged to market the new interventions.

Renaud questions a future in which health care systems are allowed to grow as they did in the 1970s and 1980s and argues that "technological innovations require some form of social control."[10] It is clear that good health requires much more than access to hospital and medical services and that the growth in expenditures on these services is relentless. It is also clear that we need to set priorities and evaluate interventions. In response to these imperatives, health reformers have developed an array of proposals for reform and restructuring to maximise population health cost-effectively.

The shape of the health care system, the evaluation of medical interventions, and the social, economic and cultural environments in which health systems operate – these are the three key areas where change is needed.

Reshaping health care

It is well over 30 years since it was recognised that health insurance, public and private, institutionalises unplanned, private medical practice and entrenches hospital-focused, technology-driven, curative medical services. Soon after national health insurance was introduced in Canada, following a long political struggle, one analyst, disappointed by the focus on sickness services in the new system, wrote:

> [W]e have committed ourselves to public payment for health services which are beyond the present public means to control and operated by professional practitioners largely in their own interest... [H]ealth remains unorganised, unplanned and fragmented... its organisational

> pattern for providing patient care is chaotic at best... [I]t is characterised by persistent shortages of personnel, an oversupply of some types of specialist practitioners and an acute shortage of others... constant conflict between medical and nonmedical practitioners and chronic maldistribution of services.[11]

Concerns of this nature were reiterated in studies undertaken in different Canadian provinces in the 1970s, particularly in the province of Quebec, and in research in many other countries.[12] They were reinforced by a broader critique of curative medicine which emerged around the same time, led by writers such as Victor Fuchs, Ivan Illich and Paul Starr.[13] In Australia, the health economist, Lou Opit, argued that:

> The view of medical care that society holds is essentially one which the medical profession has promoted... This... has led to an ideology which promotes medical care as the only good and the quality of care as being equivalent to the quantity of care... more health is the same as more medical care or even the same as more health insurance.[14]

It follows from this critique that at least some resources should be devoted to programmes and policies that will promote health and a healthy environment. Reflecting that view, a community health movement, forerunner to the women's health movement, emerged in a number of countries. Reformers argued that a strong primary health care structure, with citizen participation in decision-making, should be the basis of a modern health system – concepts pursued by the World Health Organisation in its *Health for All* strategy, published in 1978.[15]

Because practitioners in solo or even group practices cannot provide a comprehensive range of services and integrated care, any serious commitment to primary health care will involve a sweeping reorganisation of a predominantly private health care delivery system. As one primary care specialist has argued, "We're carrying the 19th-century clinical office into the 21st-century world. It's time to retire it."[16] The primary care vision is for a network of centres, rationally spread across a country, providing a comprehensive, integrated range of preventive, educational, counselling, caring and social advocacy services as well as conventional medical services. Publicly controlled centres would also open up the opportunity for citizens to participate in their own health and in the health of the environment in which they live.

Despite slow progress, some headway has been made in European countries and in parts of Canada. The best of the community health centres in the Canadian province of Quebec, for example, provide an impressive range of services, with prevention services that identify "at risk" citizens. A number of European countries have changed their delivery systems to reduce fragmentation and plan a more rational spread of services. In some countries, community members control local centres.[17]

In Australia, community health centres were established under the Whitlam government "to develop facilities and services in a coordinated manner for the provision and planning of prevention, treatment, rehabilitation and related welfare aspects of community health."[18] While these centres never attained the objectives that had been set for them, they have concentrated on the needs of the most disadvantaged groups and generated support among the people they serve. Under successive governments, however, they have been allowed to wither away.

To be effective, primary care centres need to be publicly owned and controlled; otherwise, a rational distribution of resources across the country is impossible. A planned, publicly directed set of services can overcome distribution problems. In the United States, a network of over 3000 federally funded community health centres provides a range of services, including preventive services, to low-income individuals and families in medically underserviced areas, both rural and urban, helping to overcome access problems.

Replacing private, fee-for-service medical practice with capitation, where doctors are paid a yearly fee for each person registered on their lists, or salaries would remove the incentive to overservice and reorient the system towards health. Many OECD countries have already moved away from the fee-for-service system. Remuneration changes are used to influence diagnostic use and prescribing behaviour and, in several European countries, other mechanisms are being employed to monitor treatment and practice patterns. Primary care practitioners are mostly employed on salary in Greece, Finland, Iceland, Mexico, Norway, Portugal, Spain and Turkey. Capitation systems operate in Britain, Austria, Denmark, Ireland and the Netherlands, and have become more frequent under "managed" care in the United States. Sweden combines the three forms of remuneration.[19]

The evidence about the cost savings likely to accrue from the abolition of fee-for-service is inconclusive but a 2003 OECD review suggests that expenditures are higher in fee-for-service systems.[20] Gail Donner, a Canadian professor of nursing, argues that "as long as there is a group of providers who are permitted to act as entrepreneurs... distortion in the redistribution of both dollars and services will continue to be a serious problem."[21] It is worth quoting a recent OECD assessment of the implications of the fee-for-service system:

> The fee-for-service approach gives physicians full discretion over the level and mix of services, referrals, and other treatment options... doctors face incentives to expand the volume and price of services they provide. The risk of supplier induced demand is particularly strong with this type of payment system, for example, by increasing services provided "in-house" even if there would be advantages, e.g. through economies of scale, in making more use of secondary suppliers.[22]

In summary, strong arguments have emerged about the need to reform delivery systems. Comprehensive, health-oriented services are beyond the capacity of solo practitioners and an equitable distribution of personnel and resources requires public supervision and a move away from private, fee-for-service practice. A change of remuneration mode would also resolve the longstanding problem that increases in medical benefit levels in Australia are quickly absorbed in higher fees. It is more than reasonable to ask whether private medical practice is appropriate in the 21st century when 81.8 per cent of doctors' incomes are paid by the federal government directly from taxpayer funds.[23] No matter how the lily is gilded in arguments about the sanctity of doctor–patient relationships and so on, private medical practice is not private enterprise and has not been so since governments began to pay the lion's share of medical fees decades ago. Any other industry where government owns and runs most of the infrastructure (public hospitals), pays for training and provides 81.8 per cent of income would be called a "public service."

Evaluating interventions

Internationally, a lively discussion has emerged about the need to evaluate the effectiveness of health services, treatments and technologies. Evaluation is seen as crucially important in the context of budgetary restraint and quality of care. If the significant chunk of national income invested in health is to be spent wisely on health-enhancing as well as curative services, and if governments are to be able to control costs, it is imperative that money is not wasted on useless or even harmful interventions. Evaluation is also critically important from a quality-of-care perspective: studies in the United Kingdom, the United States, Australia and Denmark have revealed high annual death rates due to medical errors.[24] Although controversial and still fraught with methodological difficulties, evaluation of both medical effectiveness and cost effectiveness is poised to become an integral part of modern health care systems.

In times gone by, evaluation was largely left to a self-regulating medical profession but because – in the words of the health services researcher Manoa Renwick – "a great deal of medical practice lacks a rigorous scientific basis and depends largely on unsystematic observation method," there is enormous variation in treatments and practices.[25] The Australian health economist, the late Sidney Sax, has argued that the evaluation of many therapeutic and surgical innovations has been "haphazard" in Australia and that some medical services are offered inefficiently and some are even harmful.[26] Bob Evans makes the same point for Canada.[27] Forces operate to promote the uncritical introduction of new procedures and technologies. These forces include media coverage of "breakthrough" innovations, manufacturer promotion of products, and physician and medical journal acceptance before trial results and evaluation reports are completed. In addition, there are sometimes powerful financial incentives for providers, who stand to profit through taxpayer or insurance funding of services produced on privately owned machines. Conflict of interest – a concern in many professions – is rarely investigated in medicine. Internationally, research has shown a wide variation in practice and intervention patterns but there is little evidence about effectiveness.[28] In a survey of the research, Noralou Roos and Les Roos found, for example, that Canadian rates of coronary artery bypass surgery were half those of the United States but more than twice those in Britain. Moreover, there was a greater than twofold variation in rates between cities within Canada. The problem, according to these researchers, is that no one knows whether these differences are good or bad![29] Roos and Roos found that a significant amount of intervention is inappropriate and that "both expert panels and cost effectiveness studies tend to overestimate the benefits of treatment."[30] They conclude:

> The blunt reality is that there is little hard evidence available to evaluate the effectiveness of many medical acts and procedures within or outside the acute care sector. Furthermore, this lack of evidence is pervasive. It includes everything from commonplace procedures to high-tech interventions. In the absence of such evidence, opinions within the medical profession differ widely...[31]

Under these circumstances, a strong "evidence-based medicine" or outcomes movement has emerged.[32] As Karen Davis told the US Senate inquiry, it is no longer viable "to simply pay for services rendered without establishing a scientific basis for effectiveness, not just for new drugs but for consultations, procedures, and tests."[33] Thinking in the area can be divided into two strands. One focuses on the need to evaluate interventions to determine their medical effectiveness and ensure quality of care.[34] Sidney Sax has called on colleagues in the profession to take "the lead in the evaluation of their work."[35]

The other strand of thinking is that technologies and procedures need to be evaluated not only in terms of medical effectiveness but also in terms of cost, an approach termed "economics based medicine."[36] Technologies, widely defined, should be evaluated on the basis of whether they will achieve "maximum gains in terms of population health from a finite budget," as the health economist, Alan Maynard, put it.[37] A "social ethic" is involved here: decision-making should focus on the health needs of society as a whole, rather than on the specific needs of individuals. In other words, there will be public control over the availability of interventions, and physician decisions about the best care for individual patients should be made within the context of available treatments. As Maynard argues:

> Social values must, in a publicly financed system, be balanced with clinical values to determine which patients will and will not get treatment. Neither the clinician nor the economist should dominate decisions about who will live in what degree of pain and discomfort and who, in extremis, will die.[38]

Such an approach necessarily involves rationing, an inevitable feature of modern health systems, and gives rise to a bewildering array of ethical issues. In Australia, a recent editorial in the *Medical Journal of Australia* recognised the dilemmas and argued that decisions about priorities and allocation in health will inevitably come under increasing scrutiny.[39]

Evaluation processes are under way in some European countries, particularly in the United Kingdom and France.[40] Evaluation, however, is a high-risk activity for governments because it can readily be portrayed as jeopardising treatment. According to Canadian researchers, community understanding must underpin evaluative processes:

> Government policy, public regulation, and, given the correct incentives, medical self-regulation can only proceed under assumptions and beliefs that roughly match those of the public. Effectively presenting the public with the evidence we now have on the limits to medicine and the potential of other investments in health, may be the most important element in any strategy to uncouple the medical care-health identity.[41]

Recent research shows that Australians are very keen to have their preferences considered when priorities are being set.[42]

Health in context

For more than a century, research has shown a close association between social deprivation and ill health. In 1980, the Black Report found serious inequalities in health outcomes in Britain.[43] In 1992, the National Health Strategy revealed a similar situation in Australia, with Aboriginal people having particularly poor outcomes.[44] Recent research in the United States shows that men with family incomes in the top 5 per cent of income distribution can expect to live for about 25 per cent longer than those in the bottom 5 per cent.[45] Recent British research suggests that the health gap between the top and bottom social groups is becoming wider and that the difference can mean that wealthy people live ten or more years longer.[46] Marc Renaud summarises the evidence:

> [H]ealth derives from our ability to adapt... From the friendship and support networks to which we have access at work, at home, and in the community. Health also stems from... some control over our work, and from a capacity for dealing with abrupt changes in our lives (unemployment, separation, death, etc)... The largest gap lies between the richest and the poorest. But the middle classes are also affected. The lower one is situated in the social hierarchy as defined by work, lodging, education, income, the lower one's probability of staying in good health and the lower one's life expectancy. This is the most frequent and most pervasive of all the observations made in the history of public health research.[47]

This knowledge forms the foundation of what has become known as a "multifactorial"– or "healthy public policy" – approach, first set out in the Lalonde Report in Canada in 1974 and integral to the World Health Organisation's *Health for All* strategy and the Ottawa Charter for Health Promotion of 1986. Advocates of healthy public policy want to see resources devoted to reducing deprivation by increasing education and income levels, providing a comprehensive range of public services and improving the physical environment.

Apart from the political problem that a healthy public policy would disturb existing power structures, there is also uncertainty in the literature about just where resources might most profitably be assigned. While the link between socioeconomic status and health is beyond doubt, the specific ways that deprivation translates into ill health remain unclear. This presents something of a problem for those charged with designing practical programs and deciding which risk factors need attention, particularly since the evidence suggests that real results require action at multiple levels. Nevertheless, a growing body of knowledge is accumulating and successful programs have been implemented.[48]

Progress has been slow, however. A World Health Organisation report suggests that policy-makers "may have been thwarted by existing configurations of power and resources."[49] The North American health analysts, Theodore Marmor, Morris Barer and Robert Evans, come to the same conclusion, arguing that significant reforms can only come after there has been a "modification of a nation's underlying belief system" about health.[50] This belief system is particularly hard to change where powerful medical organisations uphold established ideas and resist change. As they see it, the health paradigm is one that "assigns a central role to medical care in combating disease." The paradigm is:

> embodied in what has become the largest single industry in the OECD world. This concentration of economic power and (with it) political influence must, and does, resist significant change in the supporting system of beliefs.[51]

Without wide debate and rigorous information and evidence, belief systems will change very slowly, if at all. Citizens will be influenced by opinion leaders, many of whom have a vested interest in the status quo. In Australia, public debate rarely includes health system issues, with a few sporadic exceptions. In contrast to other countries, there have been no major inquiries into the health system, except for the National Health Strategy of the early 1990s, which was largely ignored by opinion leaders. Indeed, Australia, for all its changes of policy direction, has never had a major inquiry into health financing. Policy-making has taken place largely behind closed doors and citizens have little choice but to accept the outcomes. The central question – how priorities should be set in order to maximise the effectiveness of the considerable share of national wealth devoted to medical care – is not debated. Instead, we have a rather unedifying scramble for advantage.

CHAPTER 8

The future of universality

When governments extend an open hand to private health care entrepreneurs as typified in the US, there is a double consequence. They effectively deinsure a range of citizens... and they substitute the sometime inefficiency of public insurance for the unproductive overhead of private profit!

– Daniel Drache and Terry Sullivan, 1999

Why has the Howard government persisted so single-mindedly with privatisation in the face of decades of international evidence showing that private health insurance systems only work at the expense of access and cost control? Why has it pursued its policies in the face of widespread support for Medicare, strong opposition to privatisation and evidence that the principles of Medicare are basically sound? The inherent contradictions that the Coalition's policies have created ensure continuing instability. The government will be forced to make difficult choices between further privatisation and even larger increases in its own outlays. And what policy direction will the Labor Party pursue? Will it retain its long commitment to universality or will it, too, try to preside over a precarious set of arrangements in which the only certainties are poor outcomes for Medicare patients and enduring political strife.

Past Australian experience shows that it is impossible to maintain a stable balance between the public and private financing sectors in a mixed, two-tiered system. The Fraser government was unable to stabilise the relative market shares of the private sector and Medibank because, as private-sector costs rose, people moved back to Medibank.

An almost identical process is under way at the moment. The cost of private insurance premiums is rising steadily. Private health insurance coverage began to decline very soon after its peak of 45.7 per cent in September 2000. By March 2002, it had fallen to 44.6 per cent and by September 2003 to 43.3 per cent. As costs increase or if there is an economic downturn, this decline will accelerate. The federal government will have to increase its own expenditures to boost the rebate or invent some other mechanism to force people into private insurance. Alternatively, it could let services under Medicare deteriorate even further. Each of these options is politically dangerous.

Under the circumstances, the only reasonable explanation of the policy course taken by the Howard government is that it is motivated by ideological concerns – concerns that fit firmly within Liberal Party tradition and conform closely to the thrust of Coalition policy before the 1996 "change of mind" on Medicare. In explaining policy changes, it has been the prime minister, rather than his health minister, who has often taken the lead, which suggests that the leader has strong views on the issue. It was the prime minister and not the health minister at the time, Kay Patterson, who flagged the main Fairer Medicare changes at a press conference in early 2003, a month before the formal announcement, and then appeared on national programs such as the ABC's *7.30 Report* to defend the proposals.[1] And it was the prime minister rather than Senator Patterson's successor, Tony Abbott, who announced Medicare Plus in November 2003.

Tracy Schrader from the Doctors Reform Society has gathered together the prime minister's public pronouncements on health financing during his career to reveal a long-standing, strongly worded opposition to national health insurance. She points out that Mr Howard was the treasurer in the Fraser government, which completely dismantled Medibank. At various times, the prime minister has described bulk billing as "scandalous" and "an absolute rort," and Medicare variously as a "miserable cruel fraud," a "financial monster" and a "total and complete failure." John Howard has argued that bulk billing should be confined to holders of Health Care Cards with others required to pay whatever fees doctors determine. He has argued, too, that only pensioners and the disadvantaged should be eligible for prepaid hospital care.[2] The former health minister, Kay Patterson, claimed to support Medicare, as does the present minister. But it is instructive to note Senator Patterson's response to the Doctors Reform Society: according to that organisation, health ministers "of all political persuasions" had received complimentary copies of *New Doctor*, the society's journal, for decades. Senator Patterson's office, however, returned its copies, with a note saying never to send another.[3]

Although the prime minister may have given the impression of having changed his long-standing views, he set the record straight in 2001. During the election campaign, he told journalists that the introduction of Medibank in the 1970s had been a "cardinal mistake." In his view, the old system worked well for 90 per cent of the population and special arrangements should have been made for those who were left out. Instead:

> we turned the whole thing on its head and we have never been the same since. In the process, we destroyed the honorary system and we dismantled a perfectly functioning health system. You can't go back to it... You get a new generation with different attitudes, different values.[4]

There is also a pragmatic reason for the Coalition's choice of policy direction. Private financing is of most benefit to the well-off, the Coalition's traditional constituency, because it is regressive. As discussed above, tax financing maintains the principle of contribution according to income, whereas user charges and insurance premiums are levied at a flat rate and constitute a larger proportion of income for the less well-off. Because the poor are less healthy, a shift from tax funding to private financing represents a transfer of costs from the healthy and wealthy to the poor and the sick, as Canada's Robert Evans has argued. The Coalition has a long history of providing generous public subsidies to better-off members of the community, while choosing to ignore the circumstances of the most needy groups, a tendency demonstrated in research on the Menzies and Fraser eras.[5] The Howard government's health policies follow in this tradition.

Medicare came with all manner of imperfections. It was never a fully universal system. A combination of the constitutional clause prohibiting "civil conscription" and the opposition of most branches of the medical profession created political obstacles which the government of the day was not prepared to confront. So bulk billing was never compulsory. Nor did Medicare alter private fee-for-service medicine, except inside the public wards of public hospitals where medical practice was placed on a salaried or sessional basis. User charges were always an element of the system but bulk billing was put in place and, as intended, it gradually expanded to cover most medical services. Nor did Medicare institute strong cost control measures on the medical side, such as the "caps" on total expenditures for physicians' fees that are in place in Canada and other countries. But, as John Deeble has argued, the operation of the Medicare fee schedule kept downward pressure on medical fees.[6] The problem with this, from a consumer perspective, is that the tighter the control over fee schedules, the more user charges are likely to be invoked to maintain physician incomes. Moreover, the range of services covered by Medicare is extremely narrow.

Despite its shortcomings, Medicare was financially stable and mechanisms were in place for an incremental shift towards the full public funding of hospital and doctor services. After eight years of privatisation, however, bulk billing has declined, co-payments have risen, Medicare users are afraid that they will not be able to get hospital services when they need them, arrangements are being made complex to the point of incomprehensibility and conflict is more intense than at any time since the settlement of the NSW doctors' strike in 1986.[7] Health spending as a proportion of GDP is higher than ever before, as we leave "average" OECD spenders behind and move towards those countries with high levels of costly private financing.

All of which was entirely predictable on the basis of international experience. The record in the United States demonstrates clearly the problems of high levels of private financing, all of which are now evident in Australia. US experience also demonstrates that cost-control mechanisms developed for the private sector do not work. Despite the very best efforts of US employers (who pay health insurance premiums for most workers) and insurance companies, various mechanisms, including "managed care," have failed to control rampant inflation in the health sector, which is predicted to increase exponentially in the next few years.

Thus we have a set of health system arrangements in Australia which are totally unsustainable in their present form, no matter how much tinkering is done at the margins and no matter which political party holds office at the Commonwealth level. The choices are to sustain the present size of the private sector with huge outlays of taxpayer money (with serious implications for equity) or to allow people to flow back to Medicare as the cost of private insurance increases. There is also the question of whether the services provided for Medicare-only patients are adequate, as public funding is used to subsidise the private sector. On the medical side, bulk billing seems certain to continue its long-term decline and general practitioners and specialists will continue charging well above the level of the schedule fee. This, too, is an unstable set of arrangements. The choice is either for user charges to continue to increase or for larger public subsidies to underpin unregulated fee levels. With no control over medical fees, future governments, like governments in the past, will find themselves increasing public subsidies only to find that user charges remain as high as ever. The system cannot work and must now be the world's most unstable, if not yet the most expensive, set of arrangements.

The solution, as experience in Canada and other OECD countries shows, is to reinstitute a fully universal national health insurance system in which the community, through its government, has control not only over levels of expenditure, but also over the kind of health care delivery system we have, the kind of technologies we choose to use and the quality of the social environment in which the health care system operates.

Will Labor, when it returns to office, put Medicare back together again? It could be that we have seen the last of the party's commitment to universality. In 2003, Labor was divided on a number of issues. Partly, this reflects the fact that state and territory governments – all of which are Labor – are concerned about falling bulk-billing rates because, as user costs rise, people are seeking medical services from the emergency departments of state-funded public hospitals. The NSW Labor government's submission to the Senate inquiry proposed that Medicare be extended to cover general medical services in emergency departments. It proposed incentives to induce people to use private hospital emergency departments and argued for more support for general practitioner services in areas where doctors are in short supply.[8] These proposals are designed to remove pressure from state budgets and are not necessarily what a federal government, even a federal Labor government, would find acceptable. In a separate disagreement in 2003, the NSW branch of the Labor Party contradicted the federal leader concerning a possible increase in the Medicare levy.

The ACT government, too, has taken a different policy direction from that of federal Labor. Territory-financed services have borne an increasing burden: since 1998–99, non-urgent services provided by ACT public hospital emergency departments have risen by 15 per cent as a result of the lowest rates of bulk billing in the country and the greatest general practitioner shortages.[9] The ACT's major recommendation is that the funds for the private health insurance rebate should be reallocated to the public hospital system. This recommendation hit the headlines not only because it is vehemently opposed by the private health industry but also because it diverges from federal Labor policy. As the ACT submission to the Senate inquiry argues, the territory has low rates of private hospital use, despite high levels of private insurance.

A swift, damning and predictable response to this recommendation came from the private health insurance industry. The proposal was "naive, ill considered and counterproductive," and would "drive older, sicker and low income people out of the private health sector almost immediately." The Australian Health Industry Association argued that the ACT proposal was evidence of "a very disturbing" direction that Labor might be taking on the rebate and it urged the federal leader to immediately disown the ACT's ill-conceived proposals and to make "a firm, binding and unequivocal commitment that under federal Labor, the rebate will remain."[10]

This exchange illustrates the political difficulties for a party proposing to withdraw a benefit in the face of strong interest group opposition and party political competition. Reports have it that the Labor Party, or sections thereof, has been considering a withdrawal of the rebate or a reduction in its level for some time. Concern has been reported within the party about the use of public money to give the privately insured quicker access to non-emergency hospital services than is available to Medicare patients. The opposition health spokesperson, Julia Gillard, has condemned the rebate as "an expensive failure" but, at other times, has resorted to the doublespeak characteristic of health policy pronouncements. At the party's 2004 conference, the new leader, Mark Latham, gave what one observer described as "his strongest signal" that

Labor would maintain the rebate. He took the opportunity to announce a proposal for a national dental scheme for low-income earners to replace the one abolished by the Howard government.[11] Indications are that, as in the 1998 and 2001 elections, Labor will choose to compete on issues other than universality.

Labor's approach is unlikely to be more attractive to voters than it was at earlier elections. People may not understand the details of the health system but they do understand what charges and waiting times mean for access to care. Opinion poll after opinion poll shows that Australians are strongly committed to Medicare and the (near) universal access that the system once provided. The Labor Party would gain from a promise to restore unimpeded access, despite the political opposition that providers and purveyors of insurance would mount. As voting at the 1993 election showed so clearly, the vast majority of Australians oppose the dismantling of Medicare. A redirection of the private health insurance rebate to the public hospital system and to other public health services could take place incrementally: eligibility for well-off citizens could be phased out gradually. Most Australians would support such a policy change, secure in the knowledge that they and their fellow citizens would be able to get the services they need through Medicare. Moreover, without going to the lengths of trying to regulate the fees that doctors charge – a long overdue reform in Australia in any case – incentives could be put in place to promote bulk billing. Higher Medicare benefits could be made available for all bulk-billed services, instead of restricting them to concession cardholders and children, as at present. No rocket science is needed: simple measures are available to reverse the trends of the Howard years.

The direct public subsidisation of private health insurance is a unique Australian creation that has enjoyed a long life and at the moment, unlike Medicare, shows no signs of dying. Perhaps the (second) last word should go to the Melbourne health economist, Jeff Richardson, for his colourful description of the privatisation measures of the Howard years:

> While the policies have successfully increased membership of private health insurance, they have created an industry which, along with the echidna and the platypus, could be the Australian entry into an

> international "Strange but True" contest. As individual and family incomes rise above the threshold, the effective price of private health insurance (direct price less subsidy less surcharge avoided) now falls and quickly becomes negative – individuals and families are effectively paid to purchase the product – they are left with a higher net income if insurance is purchased! [Private health insurance] is probably unique in the world in being supported by a subsidy which depends upon the purchase of a particular product. It is similar to the introduction of a tax on the incomes of those who fail to buy an Australian motorcar in order to promote the automobile industry.[12]

In the short term, a redirection of the rebate to the public health system and measures to promote bulk billing are necessary to restore access and to put a brake on steep and unnecessary cost increases. But in the longer term, far more radical measures will be needed to ensure sustainability. Greater public control will be required to shape and regulate what has become one of the largest sectors of modern economies, a sector in which runaway costs are a constant threat. Private, fee-for-service medical practice, a hangover from the cottage industry days of medicine, must be replaced by other methods of paying doctors, which will eliminate medical entrepreneurialism, smooth the path for a stronger focus on health and best practice medicine, and allow a rational allocation of services across regional, rural and remote areas of the nation. Strong, publicly funded community health centres will provide an infrastructure from which real health objectives can be pursued. Evaluation and regulation of new technologies must become a routine part of the system to ensure high-quality services at an affordable price. Finally, a real health system requires an investment in the social environment in which we all live. The social determinants of ill health, such as economic insecurity and ignorance, must be addressed if we want to reduce the health disparities that mean shorter lives and more sickness for those at the lower end of the socioeconomic ladder. Not only will such an investment reduce the burden of disease, it will also reduce the cost burden that high-tech medical care imposes on modern societies.

As a society, we endorse a progressive taxation system from which we provide for ourselves a basket of essential public services on the basis of ability to pay. Most Australians wish health to be included in that basket. But a few, who stand to gain from a privately financed system, do not. Under the Howard government, private pockets have become a major source of health financing, replacing tax funding, with serious implications for less well and less well-off Australians. The few have triumphed again.

Notes

Introduction

The epigraph is from Sidney Sax, *A Strife of Interests*, George Allen and Unwin, Sydney.

1 Lasswell, Harold, *Politics, Who Gets What, When, How*, Peter Smith, New York, 1950.

2 OECD Health Data, *Frequently Asked Data 2003*, at <http://www.oecd.org>.

3 SIPRI Yearbook, *Armaments, Disarmament and International Security*, Oxford University Press, Stockholm, 2003, p 353.

4 Knowles, the Hon Craig, "The Bulk Billing Decline," Media Release, 11 February 2003, at: <http://www.health.nsw.gov.au/news/2003/February/11-02-03.htm>.

5 Ramsey, Alan, "A 'Fairer' Medicare? Truth Is Howard Would Rather Have It Put Down," *Sydney Morning Herald*, 30 April 2003, p 15.

6 Newspoll, published in the *Australian*, 2–4 May 2003, available at: <http://www.newspoll.com.au>; Quiggin, John, "Voters Favour Better Services," *Australian Financial Review*, 22 May 2003.

7 Birrell, Bob, Hawthorne, Lesleyanne and Rapson, Virginia, "The Outlook for Surgical Services in Australasia," June 2003, Centre for Population and Urban Research, Monash University, typescript; Metherell, Mark, "Elective Trend Makes Surgeons Go Private," *Sydney Morning Herald*, 25 June 2003, p 3.

8 Australian Institute of Health and Welfare, *Health Expenditure Australia, 2001–02*, Health and Welfare Expenditure Series, no 17, Canberra, 2003, pp 29–32.

9 Commonwealth of Australia, *Medicare – Health Care or Welfare?*, The Senate, Canberra, 2003, pp xiii–xv, at: <http://www.aph.gov.au/Senate/committee/medicare_ctte/index.htm>.

10 *Commonwealth Parliamentary Debates*, House of Representatives, 3 December 1974, p 4476.

11 J. F. Cade, quoted in Sidney Sax, *A Strife of Interests*, op cit, p 95.

12 O'Loghlin, James, quoted in *Good Weekend*, 6 December 2003, p 35.

Chapter 1. Irreconcilable interests

The epigraph is from Evans, Robert G., "Health Care Reform: The Issue from Hell," *Policy Options*, July–August 1993, p 38.

1 OECD Health Data, *Frequently Asked Data 2003*, at <http://www.oecd.org>.

2 OECD, *Health Care Systems: Lessons from the Reform Experience*, Economics Department Working Papers, no 374, December 2003, at: <http://www.oecd.org/eco>; Terris, Milton, "The Three Worlds Systems of Medical Care: Trends and Prospects," *American Journal of Public Health*, vol 68, no 11, 1978, pp 1125–31.

3 Drache, Daniel and Sullivan, Terry, "Health Reform and Market Talk: Rhetoric and Reality," in Daniel Drache and Terry Sullivan (eds), *Health Reform: Public Success Private Failure*, Routledge, London, 1999, p 6; Evans, Robert G., "Health for All or Wealth for Some? Conflicting Goals in Health Care Reform" in Anne Mills (ed), *Reforming Health Sectors*, Kegan Paul International, London, 2002, p 31.

4 Anderson, Gerard F. et al, "It's the Prices, Stupid: Why the United States Is So Different from Other Countries," *Health Affairs*, vol 22, issue 6, 2003, p 92.

5 OECD Health Data, 2003, op cit.

6 Australian Institute of Health and Welfare, *Health Expenditure Australia, 2001–02*, Health and Welfare Expenditure Series, no 17, 2003, Canberra, p 9.

7 Macmillan, John, "Commonwealth Constitutional Power Over Health," Consumers' Health Forum of Australia, no date, pp 42–46.

8 Kewley, T. H., *Social Security in Australia, 1900–72*, 2nd edition, Sydney University Press, Sydney, 1973, p 363.

9 Quoted in ibid, pp 509–10.

10 Australian Institute of Health and Welfare, *Health Expenditure Australia, 2001–02*, 2003, op cit, p 18.

Chapter 2. Irreconcilable ideologies

The epigraph is from Liberal Party of Australia and National Party of Australia, *Policy on Health*, 1 December 1984, typescript, p 2.

1 Quoted in Gray, Gwen, "The Termination of Medibank," *Politics*, vol 19, no 2, November 1984, p 4.

2 Hunter, T., "Planning Health Policy in Australia, 1941–1945," *Public Administration*, Autumn 1966, pp 3, 22.

3 Gray, Gwen, "Reform and Reaction in Australian Health Policy," *Journal of Health Politics, Policy and Law*, vol 21, no 3, 1996, p 601.

4 Quoted in Gray, Gwendolyn, *Federalism and Health Policy*, University of Toronto Press, Toronto, 1991, pp 84–85.

5 Ibid, pp 60–62.

6 R. G. Casey quoted in T. H. Kewley, *Social Security in Australia, 1900–72*, 2nd edition, Sydney University Press, Sydney, p 159.

7 Quoted in Gray, *Federalism and Health Policy*, op cit, p 88.

8 Watts, R., "The Light on the Hill: The Origins of the Australian Welfare State, 1935–45," PhD Thesis, University of Melbourne, 1983, p 161; Sax, Sidney, *Health*

Care Choices and the Public Purse, Allen and Unwin, Sydney, 1990, pp 41–42.

9 Liberal Party of Australia and National Party of Australia, op cit, p 9.

10 Bean, Clive, "Issues in the 1993 Election," *Australian Journal of Political Science*, vol 29, Special Issue, 1994, pp 154–55.

11 Health Insurance Commission, *Annual Reports*, 1986–87, p 30, 1996–97, p 42, Health Insurance Commission, undated.

12 Nelson, Brendan, "The Government's Vision for Health Care in Australia," *Healthcover*, June–July 1997, p 37.

13 Nelson, Brendan, "Private Insurance Sensible and Vital Protection Against the Unknown," *Healthcover*, October–November 1997, p 52.

14 Ibid, p 54.

15 Hall, Jane, "Incremental Change in the Australian Health Care System," *Health Affairs*, vol 18, no 3, p 12.

Chapter 3. Irreconcilable claims

The epigraph is from Gittens, Ross, "Medicare Package's Slow Burning Fuse," *Sydney Morning Herald*, 7 May 2003, p 13.

1 Health Insurance Commission, *Annual Report*, 1997–98, Health Insurance Commission, Canberra, undated, p 19.

2 Health Insurance Commission, *Annual Report*, 1997–98, op cit, p 73.

3 Nelson, Brendan, "Private Insurance Sensible and Vital Protection Against the Unknown," *Healthcover*, October–November 1997, pp 54–57.

4 Hall, Jane, "Incremental Change in the Australian Health Care System," *Health Affairs*, vol 18, no 3, 1999, pp 95–110.

5 Private Health Insurance Administration Council, *Annual Report*, 1997–98, AGPS, Canberra, 1998.

6 *Canberra Times*, 23 May 1998, p 3.

7 Commonwealth Department of Health and Aged Care, "Lifetime Health Cover," Fact Sheet 9, Budget 1999–2000, Department of Health and Aged Care, Canberra, 1999, p 1.

8 Willcox, Sharon, "Promoting Private Health Insurance in Australia," *Health Affairs*, vol 20, no 3, 2001, p 158.

9 Butler, J., "Policy Change and Private Health Insurance: Did the Cheapest Policy do the Trick?" in Gavin Mooney and Aileen Plant (eds), *Daring to Dream: The Future of Australian Health Care*, Black Swan Press, Bentley, 2001.

10 Deeble, John, "The Private Health Insurance Rebate," Report to State and Territory Health Ministers, January 2003, Typescript, p 6.

11 Sax, Sidney, *Health Care Choices and the Public Purse*, Allen and Unwin, Sydney, 1990.

12 Gray, Gwen, "No Gaps Health Insurance: A Gain for Consumers or a

Windfall for Specialists?" *Australian Health Review*, vol 22, no 3, 1999, pp 22–24.

13 Private Health Insurance Administration Council, "Industry Statistics," Medical gap information, September 2003, at: <http://www.phiac.gov.au/statistics/medicalgapinfo/gapsep03/index.htm>.

14 Deeble, John, "The Private Health Insurance Rebate," op cit, p 8.

15 Private Health Insurance Administration Council, *Annual Report*, 2001–02, AGPS, Canberra, 2002.

Chapter 4. The bulk-billing impasse: fifty years of fighting over fees

The epigraph is from the *Sydney Morning Herald*, 12 March 1970, quoted in Kewley, T. H., *Social Security in Australia, 1900–72*, 2nd edition, Sydney University Press, Sydney, 1973.

1 Quoted in Editorial, *Sydney Morning Herald*, 6 March 2003, p 14.

2 Pollard, Ruth and Metherell, Mark, "Bulk-Billing Rates Are Collapsing, Says Poll," *Sydney Morning Herald*, 12 February 2003, p 3.

3 Elliott, Amanda, "The Decline in Bulk Billing: Explanations and Implications," *Current Issues Brief*, no 3, 2002–03, Department of the Parliamentary Library, Canberra, 2002, p 7.

4 Doctors Reform Society, Submission to Senate Select Committee on Medicare, 2003, at: <http://www.aph.gov.au/Senate/committee/medicare_ctte/index.htm>.

5 Australian Medical Association, Media Release, 10 February 2003.

6 Australian Consumers' Association, Submission to the Senate Committee on Medicare, 2 June 2003, p 6, at: <http://www.aph.gov.au/Senate/committee/medicare_ctte/index.htm>.

7 Ibid, p 6.

8 Elliott, Amanda, op cit, p 5.

9 Metherell, Mark, "Higher GP Rebates a Better Way to Save the Scheme, Says Its Creator," *Sydney Morning Herald*, 30 April 2003, p 8.

10 Doctors Reform Society, Submission to Senate Select Committee on Medicare, op cit, p 1.

11 Ibid.

12 Patterson, the Hon Senator Kay, Media Release, 28 April 2003.

13 Ibid.

14 Schrader, Tracy, "Down the Gurgler? Howard Dandles Medicare Overboard" (part 1), *New Doctor*, vol 78, 2003, p 5.

15 Deeble, John, Evidence to Senate Select Committee on Medicare, Roundtable,

21 July 2003, Senate Hansard, Canberra, p 58, at: <http://www.aph.gov.au/Senate/committee/medicare_ctte/index.htm>.

16 Commonwealth of Australia, *Medicare – Health Care or Welfare?*, The Senate, Canberra, 2003, p xii, at: <http://www.aph.gov.au/Senate/committee/medicare_ctte/index.htm>.

17 Ibid, pp xvi–xx.

18 Ibid, p xiv.

19 Howard, the Hon John, Transcript of Medicare Plus Announcement, Hungarian Community Centre, Wantirna, Melbourne, 18 November 2003, at: <http://www.pm.gov.au/news/speeches/speech575.html>.

20 Deeble, John, "Smoke and Mirrors Trick Clouds Reality of GP Safety Net for Many Patients," *Sydney Morning Herald*, 19 November 2003, p 4.

21 Gross, Paul, "Medicare Plus: More Money, but Missing the Main Debate," *On Line Opinion*, 24 November 2003, at: <http://www.onlineopinion.com.au/view.asp?article=888>.

22 Abbott, Tony, "Wider Bulk Billing No Certainty: Abbott," ABC Online, at: <http://www.abc.net.au/news/newsitems/31063469.htm>.

Chapter 5. Moving closer to America: increasing costs

The epigraph is from Drache, Daniel and Sullivan, Terry, "Health Reform and Market Talk: Rhetoric and Reality" in Daniel Drache and Terry Sullivan (eds), *Health Reform: Public Success Private Failure*, Routledge, London, 1999, p 7.

1 Evans, Robert, "Health Reform: What 'Business' Is it of Business?" in Daniel Drache and Terry Sullivan (eds), *Health Reform: Public Success Private Failure*, Routledge, London, 1999; Evans, Robert G., "Health for All or Wealth for Some? Conflicting Goals in Health Care Reform" in Anne Mills (ed), *Reforming Health Sectors*, Kegan Paul International, London, 2002; Hall, Jane, Evidence to Senate Select Committee on Medicare, Roundtable, Monday, 21 July 2003, Senate Hansard, Canberra, at: <http://www.aph.gov.au/Senate/committee/medicare_ctte/index.htm>.

2 OECD, *Health Care Systems: Lessons from the Reform Experience*, Economics Dept Working Papers, no 374, December 2003, at <http://www.oecd.org/eco>; OECD Health Data, *Frequently Asked Data 2003*, at <http://www.oecd.org>.

3 Marmor, Theodore, "Lessons from the Frozen North," *Journal of Health, Politics, Policy and Law*, vol 18, no 3, Fall, pp 763–70.

4 Hussey, P. and Anderson, G., "A Comparison of Single- and Multi-Payer Health Insurance Systems and Options for Reform," *Health Policy*, vol 66, issue 3, December 2003.

5 Evans, Robert G., *Financing Health Care: Taxation and the Alternatives*, Health Policy Research Unit, Discussion Paper Series, Centre for Health Services Policy Research, University of British Columbia, October 2000, pp 18–19.

6 Davis, Karen, "Making Health Care Affordable for All Americans," Invited

testimony before the Senate Committee on Health, Education, Labour, and Pensions, 28 January 2004, p 3, at <http://www.cmwf.org>.

7 Private Health Insurance Administration Council, Operations of the Registered Health Benefits Organisations, *Annual Report*, 2002–03, p 33; Health Insurance Commission, *Annual Report*, 2001–02, at: <http://www.hic.gov.au/annualreports/ar_0102chapter4/key_business_results.htm>.

8 Davis, Karen, op cit, pp 1–9.

9 Ibid, pp 9–16.

10 Fein, Rashi, "Universal Health Insurance – Let the Debate Resume," *Journal of the American Medical Association*, vol 290, no 6, 2003, p 818.

11 Collins, Sara, Davis, Karen and Lambrew, Jeanne, "Healthcare Reform Returns to the National Agenda: The 2004 Presidential Candidates' Proposals," The Commonwealth Fund, 6 February 2004, at <http://www.cmwf.org>.

12 Gottlieb, Scott, "Half of US Doctors Want National Health Insurance Program," *British Medical Journal*, vol 327, issue 7425, 2003, p 1187.

13 Marwick, Charles, "Report Calls for Universal Health Cover for All US Citizens," *British Medical Journal*, vol 328, issue 7432, 2004, p 128.

14 Physicians' Working Group for Single-Payer National Health Insurance, "Proposal of the Physicians' Working Group for Single-Payer National Health Insurance," *Journal of the American Medical Association*, vol 290, no 6, 2003, pp 798–805.

15 Davis, Karen, op cit, p 8.

16 Ibid, p 8.

17 Deeble, John, "The Private Health Insurance Rebate," Report to State and Territory Health Ministers, January 2003, Typescript, p 1.

18 Australian Institute of Health and Welfare, *Health Expenditure Australia, 2001–02*, Health and Welfare Expenditure Series, Number 17, Canberra, 2003, p 9.

19 Ibid.

20 Deeble, John, "Hospital Utilisation and Costs, 1982–83 to 1988–89: Some Comments," *Australian Economic Review*, 1st Quarter 1991, pp 42–43.

21 Deeble, John, "Medicare: Where Have We Been? Where Are We Going?", *Australian and New Zealand Journal of Public Health*, vol 23, no 6, 1999, pp 563–570.

22 Calculations by John Deeble, January 2002.

23 Duckett, Stephen and Jackson, Terry, "The New Health Insurance Rebate: An Inefficient Way of Assisting Public Hospitals," *Medical Journal of Australia*, vol 72, 2000, p 442.

24 Ibid.

25 Pearse, James, Mazevska, Deniza and Gibbs, Andrew, "Private Health

Insurance Reform and Population Ageing," Paper presented to the Third Health Services and Policy Research Conference, Health Services Research Association of Australia and New Zealand, 16–19 November 2003, Melbourne, p 14.

26 Ibid, pp 14–16.

27 Deeble, John, "Medicare: Where Have We Been? Where Are We Going?" op cit, p 567.

28 Calculations by John Deeble, January 2002.

29 Richardson, Jeffrey, "Financing Health Care: Short Run Problems, Long Run Options," Paper Presented to the Health Reform Forum, Melbourne Business School, Melbourne, 19 September 2002.

30 John Deeble, quoted in Ruth Pollard, "Doctors Talking Up Fees, Medicare Creator Says," *Sydney Morning Herald*, 16 July 2003, p 7.

31 Deeble, John, "The Private Health Insurance Rebate," Report to State and Territory Health Ministers, January 2003, typescript, pp 1, 8.

32 Richardson, Jeffrey, "Financing Health Care: Short Run Problems, Long Run Options," op cit.

33 McAuley, Ian, "Stress on Public Hospitals: Why Insurance Has Made It Worse," Australian Consumers' Association and the Australian Healthcare Association, 2004, at: <http://resources.dmt.canberra.edu.au/imcauley>.

34 Hurley, Jeremiah, Vaithianathan, Rhema, Crossley, Thomas and Cobb-Clark, Deborah, "Parallel Private Health Insurance in Australia: A Cautionary Tale and Lessons for Canada," Discussion Paper no 448, Centre for Economic Policy Research, Australian National University, May 2002, pp 17–18.

35 Saltman, R. and Van Otter, C., *Planned Markets and Public Competition*, Open University Press, Buckingham, 1992, p 87.

36 Deeble, John, "Financing Health Care in a Federated Mixed Economy," in Ronald Mendelsohn (ed), *Social Welfare Finance: Selected Papers*, Centre for Research on Federal Financial Relations, The Australian National University, Canberra, 1982, p 121.

37 Gray, Gwen, "The Termination of Medibank," *Politics*, vol 19, no 2, November 1984, p 7.

38 Private Health Insurance Administration Council, Media Release, 14 March 2003.

39 Ibid.

40 Quoted in Metherell, Mark, "No Escape from Health Fund Health as Cover Soars," *Sydney Morning Herald*, 15 March 2003, p 1.

41 Private Health Insurance Administration Council, Media Release, op cit.

42 OECD, *Private Health Insurance in Australia: A Case Study*, OECD Health Working Papers no 8, October 2003, pp 4, 32.

43 Ibid, p 35.

44 Ibid, p 39.

Chapter 6. Moving closer to America: decreasing access

The epigraph is from Evans, Robert G., "Health for All or Wealth for Some? Conflicting Goals in Health Care Reform" in Anne Mills (ed), *Reforming Health Sectors*, Kegan Paul International, London, 2002, pp 37.

1 Evans, Robert, "Health Reform: What 'Business' Is It of Business?" op cit, p 31.

2 Newhouse, J. P. and the Insurance Experiment Group, *Free for All? Lessons from the RAND Health Insurance Experiment*, Harvard University Press, Cambridge, 1993, p 180.

3 Richardson, Jeffrey, *The Effects of Consumer Co-Payments in Medical Care*, National Health Strategy, Background Paper no 5, Australian Government Printing Services, Canberra, 1991, p 5.

4 Stoddart, G., Barer, M. and Evans, R., *User Charges, Snares and Delusions: Another Look at the Literature*, Premier's Council on Health, Well-Being and Social Justice, Ontario, 1994, p 31.

5 Rice, T. and Morrison, K., "Patient Cost Sharing for Medical Services: A Review of the Literature and Implications for Health Care Reform," *Medical Care Review*, vol 51, no 3, 1994, p 257.

6 Studies reviewed in Richardson, Jeffrey, *The Effects of Consumer Co-Payments in Medical Care*, National Health Strategy, Background Paper no 5, Australian Government Printing Services, Canberra, 1991, pp 25–26.

7 Ministry of Health, *Taking the Pulse: The 1996/97 NZ Health Survey*, Wellington, 1999, pp 197–207; Ministry of Health, *Our Health, Our Future: The Health of New Zealanders 1999*, Wellington, 1999, pp 42–44.

8 Schoen, Cathy, Davis, Karen, DesRoches, Catherine, Donelan, Karen, Blendon, Robert and Strumpf, Erin, "Equity in Health Care across Five Nations: Summary Findings from an International Health Policy Survey," Issue Brief, The Commonwealth Fund, 2000, at: <http://www.cmwf.org/programs/international/schoen_5nat_ib_388.asp>.

9 Blendon, Robert, Schoen, Cathy, DesRoches, Catherine and Osborn, Robin, "Inequities in Health Care: A Five Country Survey," *Health Affairs*, vol 21, issue 3, 2002, pp 182–86.

10 Gabel, Jon, Claxton, Gary, Holve, Erin and Pickreign, Jeremy, "Health Benefits in 2003: Premiums Reach Thirteen-Year High as Employers Adopt New Forms of Cost Sharing," *Health Affairs*, vol 22, issue 5, 2003, p 120.

11 Ibid, p 117.

12 Bindman, Andrew and Haggstrom, David, "Small Steps or a Giant Leap for the Uninsured?" *Journal of the American Medical Association*, vol 290, no 6, p 816.

13 Marwick, Charles, "A Total of 58 million Americans Lack Health Insurance," *British Medical Journal*, vol 325, issue 7366, 2002, p 678.

14 Davis, Karen, "Making Health Care Affordable for All Americans," Invited

testimony before the Senate Committee on Health, Education, Labour, and Pensions, 28 January 2004, p 16, at <http://www.cmwf.org>.

15 Marwick, Charles, "Lack of Health Insurance Cost Up to $130 Billion in Illness and Premature Death," *British Medical Journal*, vol 326, no 7404, 2003, p 1418.

16 OECD Health Data, *Frequently Asked Data 2003*, at <http://www.oecd.org>.

17 Royal Australian College of General Practitioners, Submission to the Senate Select Committee on Medicare, 18 June 2003, at: <http://www.aph.gov.au/Senate/committee/medicare_ctte/index.htm>.

18 Blendon, Robert, Schoen, Cathy, DesRoches, Catherine and Osborn, Robin, op cit.

19 Ibid.

20 Birrell, Bob, Hawthorne, Lesleyanne and Rapson, Virginia, "The Outlook for Surgical Services in Australasia," Centre for Population and Urban Research, Monash University, typescript, June 2003; Royal Australasian College of Surgeons, "Critical Shortage," Media Release, 24 June 2003, at: <http:// www.surgeons.org/news/current_media_releases.html>.

21 Tridgell, Paul, "Private/Public Separation Rates: The Evidence for Inequity and Private Health Insurance Policy Failure," paper given to the Australian Health Care Summit, Canberra, 2003, at: <http://www.healthsummit.org.au/program.htm>; Metherell, Mark, "Uninsured Patients Left Behind," *Sydney Morning Herald*, 16 August 2003, p 7.

22 Senate Hansard, 24 November 2003, pp 17648–81; Department of the Parliamentary Library, "Distribution of Wage and Salary Income by Electorate," *Research Note*, no 9, October 2003, pp 1–2.

23 Commonwealth of Australia, "Medicare Plus: The Future for Medicare?" pp 51–52, at: <http://www.aph.gov.au/Senate/committee/medicare_ctte/index.htm>.

24 Quoted in Metherell and Rowbotham, 2003, p 1.

25 Duckett, Stephen, "Will Howard's Legacy Be the Destruction of Medicare?" *Age*, 5 March 2003, at: <http://www.theage.com.au/articles/2003/03/04/1046540186994.html>.

26 Schrader, Tracy, "Down the Gurgler? Howard Dandles Medicare Overboard" (part 2), *New Doctor*, vol 79, 2003, p 2.

27 Pollard, Ruth, "More Fears than Cheers Greet Health Package," *Sydney Morning Herald*, 29 April 2003, p 8.

28 Commonwealth of Australia, "Medicare Plus: The Future for Medicare?" op cit, pp xv, 49–51.

29 Ibid, p xv.

30 Quoted in Schubert, Misha, "No Crackdown on Specialists: Abbott," *Australian*, 12 February 2004.

31 Royal Australasian College of Physicians, Media Release, 11 March 2003.

32 Wade, Matt, "Medicare Plan Calls for End of Rebate," *Sydney Morning Herald*, 10 March 2003, p 2.

33 Doctors Reform Society, Submission to Senate Select Committee on Medicare, 2003, at: <http://www.aph.gov.au/Senate/committee/medicare_ctte/index.htm>.

34 Australian Democrats, Media Release, 2 May 2003.

35 Metherell, Mark, "Medicare Plan Fails to Woo: Poll," *Sydney Morning Herald*, 6 May 2003, p 3.

36 Riley, Mark, "Forget Tax Cuts, Coalition Voters Want Health, Education," *Sydney Morning Herald*, 20 May 2003, p 6.

37 Allison, Senator Lyn, Health Update, July 2003, p 4, at: <http://www.democrats.org.au>.

38 Royal Australian College of General Practitioners, Submission to the Senate Select Committee on Medicare, 18 June 2003, p 4, at: <http://www.aph.gov.au/Senate/committee/medicare_ctte/index.htm>.

39 Australian Medical Association, Media Release, 21 July 2003.

40 Royal Australian College of General Practitioners, Submission to the Senate Select Committee on Medicare, op cit.

41 Metherell, Mark, "Doctors' Groups Revive Call for Extra Charge," *Sydney Morning Herald*, 14 February 2003, p 4.

Chapter 7. Health: the issue that rarely rates a mention

The epigraph is from Renaud, Marc, "The Future: Hygeia Versus Panakeia" in Robert G. Evans, Morris L. Barer and Theodore R. Marmor (eds), *Why Are Some People Healthy and Others Not? The Determinants of Health of Populations*, Aldine de Gruyter, New York, 1994, pp 318, 324.

1 McGinnis, Michael, Williams, Russo and Knickman, James, "The Case for More Active Policy Attention to Health Promotion," *Health Affairs*, vol 21, issue 2, 2002, p 78; Australian Institute of Health and Welfare, *Health Expenditure Australia, 2001–02*, Health and Welfare Expenditure Series, Number 17, Canberra, 2003, p 38.

2 Australian Institute of Health and Welfare, Media Release, 13 December 2002.

3 World Health Organisation, *European Health Care Reform*, WHO Regional Publications, European Series, no 72, Copenhagen, 1997, pp 36–38; Maynard, Alan, "The Inefficiency and Inequalities of the Health Care Systems of Western Europe," *Social Policy and Administration*, vol 15, no 2, Summer 1981; Evans, Robert G., Barer, Morris L. and Marmor, Theodore R. (eds), *Why Are Some People Healthy and Others Not? The Determinants of Health of Populations*, Aldine de Gruyter, New York, 1994; Marmot, M. and Wilkinson, R. (eds), *Social Determinants of Health*, Oxford University Press, Oxford, 1999.

4 McKeown, Thomas, *The Modern Rise of Population*, Edward Arnold, London, 1976; McKeown, Thomas, *The Role of Medicine: Dream, Mirage or Nemesis?*, Nuffield Provincial Hospitals Trust, London, 1976.

5 Bunker J., Frazier H. and Mosteller, F., "The Role of Medical Care in Determining Health: Creating an Inventory of Benefits," in B. Amick et al (eds), *Society and Health*, Oxford University Press, New York, 1995.

6 Maynard, Alan, op cit; Townsend, P. and Davidson, N., *Inequalities in Health: The Black Report*, Penguin, London, 1982; Sax, Sidney, *Health Care Choices and the Public Purse*, Allen and Unwin, Sydney, 1990, pp 22–39; Abel-Smith, Brian, Figueras, Josep, Holland, Walter, McKee, Martin and Mossialos, Elias, *Choices in Health Policy, An Agenda for the European Union*, Dartmouth Publishing, Aldershot, 1995, pp 1–22; Siegrist, Johannes and Marmot, Michael, "Health Inequalities and the Psychosocial Environment – Two Scientific Challenges," *Social Science and Medicine*, vol 58, issue 8, 2004, pp 1463–73.

7 Bunker, John, "When Doctors Disagree," *New York Review of Books*, 25 April 1985, pp 7–12.

8 Renaud, Marc, "The Future: Hygeia Versus Panakeia" in Robert G. Evans, Morris L. Barer and Theodore R. Marmor (eds), *Why Are Some People Healthy and Others Not? The Determinants of Health of Populations*, op cit.

9 Clark, William R., *The New Healers: The Promise and Problems of Molecular Medicine in the 21st-Century*, Oxford University Press, New York, 1997, p viii; Mattick, John, "The Human Genome and the Future of Medicine," *Medical Journal of Australia*, vol 179, no 4, 2003, pp 212–16.

10 Renaud, Marc, op cit, p 321.

11 McLeod, Jack, "Health, Wealth, and Politics" in Laurier Lapierre et al (eds), *Essays on the Left*, McClelland and Stewart, Toronto, 1971, pp 90–91.

12 Gray, Gwendolyn, *Federalism and Health Policy*, University of Toronto Press, Toronto, 1991, pp 104–11.

13 Fuchs, Victor, *Who Shall Live: Health, Economics and Social Policy*, Basic Books, New York, 1974; Illich, Ivan, *Medical Nemesis: The Expropriation of Health*, Marion Boyars, London, 1975; Starr, Paul, *The Social Transformation of American Medicine*, Basic Books, New York, 1982.

14 Opit, Lou, "Wheeling, Healing and Dealing: The Political Economy of Health Care in Australia," *Community Health Studies*, vol 11, no 3, 1983, pp 239–40.

15 World Health Organisation, op cit, pp 233–39.

16 Donald Berwick quoted in Boddenheimer, Thomas, "Innovations in Primary Care in the United States," *British Medical Journal*, vol 326, issue 7393, 2003, p 797.

17 Gray, Gwendolyn, *Federalism and Health Policy*, op cit, pp 165–68; Abel-Smith, Brian, Figueras, Josep, Holland, Walter, McKee, Martin and Mossialos, Elias, *Choices in Health Policy, An Agenda for the European Union*, Dartmouth Publishing, Aldershot, 1995, pp 67–76.

18 Hospitals and Health Services Commission Interim Committee, *Report on a Community Health Program for Australia*, AGPS, Canberra,1973, p 28.

19 Abel-Smith, Brian, et al, op cit, pp 45–47; OECD, *Health Care Systems: Lessons from the Reform Experience*, Economics Department Working Papers, no 374, December 2003, at: <http://www.olis.oecd.org/olis/2003doc.nsf/linkto/eco-wkp(2003)28>.

20 OECD, ibid.

21 Donner, G., "Squeezing the Balloon: The Fallacy of Demand Modification," in Daniel Drache and Terry Sullivan (eds), *Health Reform: Public Success Private Failure*, Routledge, London, 1999, p 256.

22 OECD, *Health Care Systems: Lessons from the Reform Experience*, op cit, p 29.

23 Australian Institute of Health and Welfare, *Health Expenditure Australia, 2001–02*, Health and Welfare Expenditure Series, Number 17, Canberra, 2003, p 47.

24 OECD, *Health Care Systems: Lessons from the Reform Experience*, op cit, p 16.

25 Renwick, Manoa, "Doctors' Decisions and the Equity of the Health System," *Current Affairs Bulletin*, February 1991, p 29.

26 Sax, Sidney, *Health Care Choices and the Public Purse*, Allen and Unwin, Sydney, 1990, p 35.

27 Evans, Robert G., "Health Care Reform: 'The Issue from Hell'," *Policy Options*, July–August 1993.

28 OECD, *Health Care Systems: Lessons from the Reform Experience*, op cit; Sax, Sidney, op cit, pp 111–13.

29 Roos, N. and Roos, L., "Small Area Variations, Practice Style and Quality of Care" in Robert G. Evans, Morris L. Barer and Theodore R. Marmor (eds), *Why Are Some People Healthy and Others Not? The Determinants of Health of Populations*, Aldine de Gruyter, New York, 1994, p 238.

30 Ibid, p 246.

31 Ibid, p 232.

32 World Health Organisation, op cit, pp 203–14.

33 Davis, Karen, "Making Health Care Affordable for All Americans," Invited testimony before the Senate Committee on Health, Education, Labour, and Pensions, 28 January 2004, p 15, at: <http://www.cmwf.org>.

34 OECD, *Health Care Systems: Lessons from the Reform Experience*, op cit, pp 15–17.

35 Sax, Sidney, op cit, p 127.

36 Maynard, Alan and Bloor, Karen, "Dilemmas in Regulation of the Market for Pharmaceuticals," *Health Affairs*, vol 22, issue 3, 2003, p 31.

37 Maynard, Alan, "Evidence Based Medicine: An Incomplete Method for Informing Treatment Choices," *Lancet*, vol 349, 1997.

38 Ibid, p 128.

39 Editorial, *Medical Journal of Australia*, vol 179, 20 October 2003, p 396.

40 OECD, *Health Care Systems: Lessons from the Reform Experience*, op cit, pp 41–44; World Health Organisation, op cit, p 212.

41 Lomas, J. and Contandriopoulos, A-P., "Regulating Limits to Medicine: Towards Harmony in Public- and Self-Regulation" in Robert G. Evans, Morris L. Barer and Theodore R. Marmor (eds), *Why Are Some People Healthy and Others Not? The Determinants of Health of Populations*, Aldine de Gruyter, New York, 1994, p 282.

42 Wiseman, V., Mooney, G., Berry, G. and Tang, K., "Involving the General Public in Priority Setting: Experiences from Australia," *Social Science and Medicine*, vol 56, issue 5, 2003.

43 Department of Health and Social Security, *Inequalities in Health: Report of a Research Working Group* (the Black report), HM Stationary Office, London, 1980.

44 National Health Strategy, *Enough to Make You Sick: How Income and Environment Affect Health*, Research Paper no 1, September 1992.

45 Deaton, Angus, "Policy Implications of the Gradient of Health and Wealth," *Health Affairs*, vol 21, issue 2, 2002, pp 13–21.

46 Kmietowicz, Zosia, "Gap Between Classes in Life Expectancy is Widening," *British Medical Journal*, vol 327, July 2003, p 68; World Health Organisation, op cit, p 37.

47 Renaud, Marc, op cit, p 322.

48 Canadian Institute for Health Information, *Policy Approaches to Address the Impact of Poverty on Health*, Ottawa, 2003; Marmot, Michael, "The Influence of Income on Health: Views of an Epidemiologist," *Health Affairs*, vol 21, issue 2, 2002; Deaton, Angus, op cit.

49 World Health Organisation, op cit, p 36.

50 Marmor, T., Barer, M. and Evans, R., "The Determinants of a Population's Health: What Can Be Done to Improve a Democratic Nation's Health Status?" in Robert G. Evans, Morris L. Barer and Theodore R. Marmor (eds), *Why Are Some People Healthy and Others Not? The Determinants of Health of Populations*, Aldine de Gruyter, New York, 1994.

51 Ibid, p 219.

Chapter 8. The future of universality

The epigraph is from Drache, Daniel and Sullivan, Terry, "Health Reform and Market Talk: Rhetoric and Reality" in Daniel Drache and Terry Sullivan (eds), *Health Reform: Public Success Private Failure*, Routledge, London, 1999, p 7.

1 Metherell, Mark, "No Escape from Health Fund Health as Cover Soars," *Sydney Morning Herald*, 15 March 2003, p 1.

2 Schrader, Tracy, "Down the Gurgler? Howard Dandles Medicare Overboard" (part 1), *New Doctor*, vol 78, 2003, p 2.

3 Editorial, *New Doctor,* no 79, at: <http://www.drs.org.au/new_doctor/79/Editorial79.htm>

4 *Sydney Morning Herald,* 27 October 2004.

5 See, for example, Gray, Gwen, "Social Policy" in Scott Prasser, John Nethercote and John Warhurst (eds), *The Menzies Era,* Hale and Iremonger, Sydney, 1995.

6 Deeble, John, "Medicare: Where Have We Been? Where Are We Going?" *Australian and New Zealand Journal of Public Health,* vol 23, no 6, 1999, p 565.

7 For a discussion of the tortuous details of safety nets, see Deeble, John, Submission to the Senate Committee on Medicare, December 2003, at: <http://www.aph.gov.au/Senate/committee/medicare_ctte/index.htm>.

8 Government of New South Wales, Submission to the Senate Committee on Medicare, 2003, p 4.

9 ACT Government Submission to the Senate Select Committee on Medicare, 2003, pp 3–6.

10 Australian Health Industry Association, "ACT Move on Rebate Counter-Productive," Media Release, 29 July 2003.

11 Metherell, Mark, "Rebate Stays, Dental Scheme Makes Comeback," *Sydney Morning Herald,* 31 January–1 February 2004, p 11.

12 Richardson, Jeffrey, "Financing Health Care: Short Run Problems, Long Run Options," Paper Presented to the Health Reform Forum, Melbourne Business School, Melbourne, 19 September 2002, pp 5–6.

3 SJCD 00321 849G